"Jazz is born of diversity; it requires *openness*. It's a shared improvisational thread that can overcome bigotry and unite all who embrace it. In these pages, William G. Carter—who cheekily confesses that he was put on Earth to 'pray the piano'—rhapsodizes about the timeless euphoria of wholly embracing a transformative jazz performance. He's a born raconteur; readers from every walk of life will enjoy his sublime gift for sharing the jazz world's most uplifting and provocative stories, and for gently reminding us of music's power for spiritual healing."

—**Derrick Bang,** author of *Vince Guaraldi at the Piano*

"The stories, insightful connections to theological thought and spiritual experience, and unabashed passion of *Thriving on a Riff* will be memorable music to your soul. Take your time and savor; there is vibrant reflective inspiration here. Moreover, I take personal joy in knowing that this fine, meaningful offering adds more fuel to the fire of a belief I have held for many years: jazz is the exclamation point to the Resurrection!"

—**Kirk Byron Jones,** author of *The Jazz of Preaching: How to Preach with Great Freedom and Joy* and *The Spiritual Treasure of Jazz: Wisdom That Will Make Your Life Swing!*

"If you've ever wondered how jazz and authentic spirituality generate both joy and truth, this book's for you. In *Thriving on a Riff*, Bill Carter writes as a jazz musician and a pastor with a keen sense of spirituality. Bearing in mind Saint Irenaeus (second century)—'the glory of God is a human being fully alive'—Carter gives us an astonishing tour of a 'Who's Who' of great jazz musicians. Their stories reveal the depth of their own wrestling with angels and demons. What emerges in these pages is a polyphonic account of how jazz and deep spirituality keep remarkably demanding close company.

"This book is no less than a love song to the art and genius of improvisation. But it is also a musical primer about transcendence and the risks of biblical faith. Along the way we overhear the author's own listening and playing. What do prophecy, ecstasy, wisdom, and good jazz have in common? These pages give us teasing, provocative access to the answer. The pleasure here is that the words read like jazz sounds. Should you not be a jazz fan, or perhaps a spiritual skeptic, Carter's book may just change your mind. But if you love jazz and seek a deep sense of what is spiritual, this is a feast."

—**Don E. Saliers,** professor of theology and liturgy, emeritus, Emory University, coauthor of *A Song to Sing, A Life to Live* with daughter Emily of the Indigo Girls

"If you've ever been moved by music . . . improvised ways to enliven your soul . . . pull up a chair, pour yourself a drink, and dive in to *Thriving on a Riff.* This is prayer."

—**Diane Stephens Hogue,** spiritual director and former convener, Liturgy & Spirituality Seminar Group, North American Academy of Liturgy

"This is a lovely, personal, and highly readable book. The poetic 'Improvisations' along the way give good flavor to the whole, moving it more toward the world of music than simply print."

—**Jamie Howison,** author of *God's Mind in That Music: Theological Explorations through the Music of John Coltrane*

"If you consider yourself to be 'spiritual,' and if you have any interest in music—especially the sublime and moving genre of jazz—you must read this masterpiece of a book. Bill Carter has lived at the intersection of the Spirit and jazz for years, and now he shares captivating stories and illuminating insights that can challenge and form our faith in deeper, richer, more melodious ways. Bravo, maestro!"

—**Rev. Peter M. Wallace,** author of *A Generous Beckoning* and other books, and emeritus host of the *Day1* radio/podcast program

THRIVING ON A RIFF

THRIVING ON A RIFF

WILLIAM G. CARTER

JAZZ AND THE SPIRITUAL LIFE

BROADLEAF BOOKS
MINNEAPOLIS

THRIVING ON A RIFF
Jazz and the Spiritual Life

Library of Congress Cataloging-in-Publication Data

Names: Carter, William G., author.
Title: Thriving on a riff : jazz and the spiritual life / William G. Carter.
Description: Minneapolis : Broadleaf Books, 2024. | Includes bibliographic references.
Identifiers: LCCN 2023022577 (print) | LCCN 2023022578 (ebook) | ISBN 9781506497600 (hardcover) | ISBN 9781506498058 (ebook)
Subjects: LCSH: Jazz—Religious aspects.
Classification: LCC ML3921.8.J39 C38 2024 (print) | LCC ML3921.8.J39 (ebook) | DDC 201/.678165—dc23/eng/20230621
LC record available at https://lccn.loc.gov/2023022577
LC ebook record available at https://lccn.loc.gov/2023022578

Cover design: 1517 Media

Print ISBN: 978-1-5064-9760-0
eBook ISBN: 9781-5064-9805-8

Printed in China.

CONTENTS

CONTENTS

INTRODUCTION

Counting Off the Tempo

The door on the minivan opened, and Ron Vincent, our effervescent drummer, climbed in. Last to arrive after our evening concert, he was euphoric. "We were hitting it tonight," he said, "and I feel good."

Tony Marino, a bassist of few words, smiled and added, "It was a great gig."

My jazz quartet was winding up a weeklong tour of concerts. I was feeling good myself, appreciative that I may be the only Presbyterian minister who takes vacation time to go on the road with his band. I thanked them for making the trip.

"You know," said Ron, "there's something profound about this music. Something deeply spiritual. Bill, you should write a book about it."

***

Spiritual is a slippery word. I've never quite known how to define it. For many, *spiritual* points to emotional experience, evoking responses ranging from pathos to ecstasy. A soulful song resonates with the broken heart. A freewheeling improvisation evokes cheers. The skilled jazz musician can set the emotional thermostat of a room. Those who listen with available hearts can be deeply affected, even strangely warmed.

And there's something intellectual about jazz too. Complex harmonies dance between tension and release. Melodies unfold over fascinating rhythms. Musicians in this groove embrace a long tradition of theoretical knowledge and practical wisdom.

Emotional *and* intellectual, jazz connects the head and heart, suggesting a more inclusive way to plumb the depths of heaven and earth. A creative imagination unites with tapping feet. It's bothand. If jazz is *spiritual*, it does not lift us off the ground, detaching us from the hard realities of life. The music's spiritual power is a holy animation in the thick of real life. Sloth is shaken awake. Honesty smashes through denial. Static situations are cracked open to new possibilities for the fullness of life. As one saxophonist slyly affirmed, "I have a ministry of raising the dead." Jazz becomes a highway for the Holy, the Mystery, the Spirit at the heart of all things. And it can provide healing for our hearts and integration for our souls.

Integration? I know it firsthand. I live between two statues in my pastoral study. One depicts Moses holding the Ten Commandments, affirming my ongoing work as a minister. Moses stands tall, presiding over a large bookshelf of Bible commentaries, a theological dictionary, and volumes written in Greek and Hebrew.

The other statue sits across the room on the windowsill. It portrays a clown playing the piano. When this one catches my eye, I remember the hundreds of nights I have spent as a jazz pianist in clubs and concert halls—and now churches.

Against the advice of some, I have never let go of either statue. They form a set of parentheses around my life. They provide balance for my soul.

When I began to study for the ministry, I was a professional musician, the only student in my seminary class who had the distinction of playing in most of the Elks Clubs of upstate New York. I assumed music would go on the shelf when I completed my studies and entered the ministry.

But then the moment came on the day when I was invited to take the pastoral job that I've had for over thirty years. Someone in the back of the church stood up and said, "We have heard you preach, and that was pretty good. Play something for us on the piano!"

I froze, then muttered something like, "That's not why I'm here."

His response: "That's what you think."

It was an invitation to integration, a summons to weave together disparate strands of my experience. As I stomped out a rollicking version of "Amazing Grace," I did not realize I was launching on the trajectory that led to this book. Neither did I know I was beginning a journey to weave my passion for jazz with the spiritual life.

And it is a spiritual *life*. Not merely *faith*, defined as an alignment of the heart. Neither is it *religion*, which suggests venerable altars with lots of behavioral rules. Faith and religion have shaped my identity and moral foundation, but music invites me to go deeper into the Mystery that we never quite capture in religious language. The dissonant tones offer a prophetic nudge toward justice. The harmonic resolutions offer healing. One friend summarizes it by declaring, "God is in the music." Her soul is full. She's committed to justice and human harmony. There is holiness in her eyes.

One size doesn't fit all. Sometimes the spiritual life is as ecstatic as a Keith Jarrett piano concert, with back-bending gyrations and groans of delight. Other times, it is as quiet and still as Bill Evans improvising his well-known "Peace Piece" for seven minutes on two chords. In the thick of such moments, we may discern evidence of divine activity in a musical art form. Perhaps we will discover how jazz can inform, and connect to, the life of the Spirit.

This is my invitation to you. How might music awaken, enrich, and empower our lives and direct us toward acts of love, justice, and mercy? That's what interests me, and we have an extraordinary jazz tradition to offer many clues and connections. It intersects with the wisdom of the ancient Saint Irenaeus, who famously quipped, "The glory of God is a human alive."

Let's see if jazz can bring us alive. Completely alive.

CHAPTER ONE

THE WOW MOMENT

The Possibility of Sonic Transcendence

> God? Well, I don't know about God. But I believe in Louis Armstrong.
>
> —*Loren Schoenberg*

CAN ANYTHING HAPPEN ON
A THURSDAY NIGHT?

The Latonia Theater was buzzing that Thursday in Oil City, Pennsylvania. Betsy fidgeted in her balcony seat. For the first time, she was going to hear a concert by the legendary jazzman Louis Armstrong. Her aunt Mamie had bought two balcony seats for them to celebrate her nineteenth birthday. Betsy didn't know much about Louis or his music, but her family had listened to plenty of jazz on the family radio and phonograph.

After the crowd filled the hall, the announcer introduced Louis Armstrong and his All-Stars: Barney Bigard on clarinet, Trummy Young on trombone, Billy Kyle on piano, Arvell Shaw on bass, Barrett Deems on drums, and the formidable Velma Middleton on vocals. The band kicked into their theme song, "When It's Sleepy Time Down South," and a cheer went up from the audience.

Music filled the hall, and the crowd began to sway. When Trummy Young stepped up to blow a trombone solo, everybody cheered, so he dug in harder. Bigard's clarinet performed tricks that Betsy, an all-state clarinetist in high school, could not have even imagined. But the best part of the show was Louis "Pops" Armstrong, with his effervescent smile and boundless musical energy. The man created joy. And the audience wouldn't let him stop.

To this day, Betsy vividly remembers two things about that show: First, there was a stack of folded handkerchiefs on top of the piano. As Armstrong blew his trumpet, his brow began to glisten. Drops of hard-earned perspiration were visible from the balcony. Pops frequently took a handkerchief from the stack, mopped his scalp, and dropped it on the floor of the stage. Soon, he would grab another handkerchief, wipe his brow again, and drop it on the floor.

The second thing Betsy remembers is what Pops did to that room. The excitement was palpable. You could taste the joy in the air. All 1,600 seats were full, quite a feat for a Thursday night in northwestern Pennsylvania, and by Betsy's description, everybody in that auditorium was thoroughly, completely alive.

***

That concert at the Latonia Theater took place on March 31, 1955, and yet, almost seventy years later, my mother tells that story as if it happened last night. "I was there," Betsy says, almost reverentially.

Something happened the first time my mother heard Louis Armstrong jazz up a room. Listening to her describe it, you'd think she was describing a spiritual experience. A "wow" moment. Her heart was touched in an emotional moment. Yet it was more than an emotional and spiritual event. It was fully physical. Her right ankle was sore from tapping her foot fiercely. "I didn't even know I was doing it."

It was also a communal moment, one of those rare events when people are connected. Strangers were smiling at one another. Differences were transcended. Irrespective of where the members of the audience might scatter to after the conclusion of the show, they had held an hour and a half of music in common. They talked about it at dinner tables and by office water coolers. A few are still talking about it decades later.

But it wasn't just happiness that was felt that night. Sure, the band played its share of happy songs, but they also lamented in the language of the blues. Armstrong had a setlist in those years that mixed up the order of his tunes: fast, slow, sweet, sad. It was a full palette of the human experience. This is what she meant when she said the crowd was thoroughly, completely alive.

Music like that can be released as incense in a room. In those remarkable moments, people have the potential to be transformed. If an audience member arrives bearing a burden, the difficulty can be dropped to the floor like one of Armstrong's handkerchiefs. This casting aside of troubles does not mean to insinuate that our burdens are any less significant. Rather, it suggests there is more to life than pain and suffering.

In those moments, you are completely alive.

SOMETHING BEYOND EXPRESSION

These are moments of deep reality. They come in music halls or on mountaintops, in the woods, or on the stage. No one has words adequate to describe them, although novelist and spiritual writer Madeleine L'Engle describes such occasions as points of reality opening—moments of awe, clarity, and truth. The theater curtains pull apart for a brief time, and we get a glimpse of what is truly happening. We hear the music that had previously been muted. We encounter *Reality* with a capital R.

One of these classic moments in the spiritual tradition, L'Engle notes, is the strange occasion when Jesus took three of his disciples to the top of a mountain. While standing closer to heaven, Jesus suddenly began to shine as bright as the sun. Peter, James, and John could not capture the moment, and neither can the storytellers who report it. It is quite possible that one of the Gospel writers made up the word *transfiguration* to describe this scene that evades description.

These moments are pregnant with the possibility of abundant life, even if we push against them. L'Engle writes, "We are afraid of the Transfiguration for much the same reason that people are afraid that theater is a 'lie,' that a story isn't 'true,' that art is somehow immoral, carnal, and not spiritual . . . (but) as a child, it did not seem strange to me that Jesus was able to talk face to face with Moses and Elijah, the centuries between them making no difference."

I can't help but wonder if music provides a conduit for God to break down the barriers that otherwise obscure our view of the divine. What if, like the transfiguration, eternity smashes all the clocks so that the past and future coincide in a single moment? What if God sneaks up on us in places we would never expect God to make an appearance—mountaintops, concert auditoriums, even churches? What if holiness happened right here, right now, in a moment beyond words? It could be frightening.

When these moments come, our human tendency is to attempt to explain them as a way of managing them, controlling them, reducing them, or dismissing them. How many times has a brilliant sunset spoken beyond words, yet we shrug it off seconds later? How often are we given a glimpse of great glory, only to respond by trying without success to capture it on our cameras or phones? Or how often have we experienced a moment like my mother did, that night in Oil City, Pennsylvania, when Louis Armstrong blew vitality into the room through his trumpet? The tragedy is that when we don't know what to do with the feelings evoked by the experience, we move on, forgetting how close we've come to experiencing the divine.

On the Mount of Transfiguration, the disciple Peter vainly tried to capture the moment. "Lord," he said to Jesus, "let me build three monuments to this moment." This hardly ever works.

On a family vacation, I stood on the edge of the Grand Canyon and tried to snap a picture of it. The photograph turned out significantly smaller than the venue.

Even that great Louis Armstrong concert cannot be replicated. I was excited to find a concert recording from around the time when my mother saw him perform. I listened with anticipation, but so much of the juice of presence was gone. Notoriously, the experience is never the same.

Spiritual moments are unmanageable. They slip away like incense evaporates into the air, like a sound trailing in the distance.

But they are real. Oh, are they real.

***

Jazz has the power to raid the inarticulate. Something happens. A glimpse of transcendence, an opening up to what no one could have imagined.

Shortly after pianist McCoy Tyner passed away in March 2020, bassist Christian McBride recalled a moment they had shared during a weeklong booking at Yoshi's, a club in Oakland, California. Tyner had booked McBride and drummer Lewis Nash for a six-night run. As is typical for musicians of that caliber, preparations were minimal. They met to talk through a couple of unfamiliar tunes, counted off a few tempos, and then slipped offstage before the doors opened. McBride describes what happened next:

> When we started the gig that night, a spirit took hold of Mr. Tyner—and us—that I can't say I'd felt before or since. Forget about feel, you could almost SEE fire, wind, and rain coming out of the piano that night. When we finished the first set, Lewis and I were DRENCHED in sweat. Our suits were ruined. We just looked at each other and thought, "What just happened?" McCoy just sat there peaceful as could be, sweetly giggling at me and Lewis' amazement. The same thing happened in the second set.

Those who were blessed to be present for those moments could not find the words to describe what happened that evening. After the concert, Geoffrey Keezer, another notable pianist, came backstage, fighting back tears. He could only stammer, "I'm not sure I have ever heard McCoy Tyner play like *that*." As McBride put it, "This gig wasn't simply a gig; it was an experience. The whole week was like that."

Jazz opens those wow moments, where the engagement is in the spirit and in the body: fire, wind, and rain. Those are the moments that the psalms speak to, built in meter and sound, and play and lament. Still, scripture doesn't comment too much on those musical moments, although one scene of musicians getting out of hand has a recognizable ring. In 1 Samuel, Saul is secretly anointed as the first king of Israel. As he's being anointed by the prophet Samuel, Saul is told he will encounter an odd group of musicians:

> After that you shall come to Gibeath-elohim (literally "hill of God"), at the place where the Philistine garrison is; there, as you come to the town, you will meet a band of prophets coming down from the shrine with harp, tambourine, flute, and lyre playing in front of them; they will be in a prophetic frenzy. Then the spirit of the LORD will possess you, and you will be in a prophetic frenzy along with them and be turned into a different person. Now when these signs meet you, do whatever you see fit to do, for God is with you.

Harp, tambourine, flute, and lyre—with frenzy and spirit? Sounds like the very first jazz quartet.

What follows is an amazing scene. The prophet-musicians truly get out of hand. They do not strum soft chords on guitars with benign smiles. No, this is a band of itinerant prophets, consumed by the visceral power of their music. Even within shouting distance of the garrison of their enemies, they are told to go with it and enter the frenzy. They follow the directive and refuse to play it safe.

As they make their music, God is within it. God is with them. And the prophet warns Saul (to assuage the fright that might come), "When you hear it, the spirit of the Lord will possess you, and you will be turned into a different person." That's the kind of power music has, unless we turn it down or turn it off, unless we consciously choose not to allow it to change us.

Time after time in scripture, God wakes us with a start. Recall the day of Christian Pentecost, when God blew breath on a gathered people, breathing the Christian Church into being, and the faithful sputtered in ecstasy.

Go to the stone cathedrals these days—the church down the block, perhaps—and they may feel like mausoleums, even as God pounds the drum in Ghana.

Why are we so afraid of visceral religion? Is the wattage too high? Does passion encroach too closely? Are we suspicious of joy?

Have we ceased to hope for the very things that could bring us alive?

***

My own encounters with music are similar to that of King Saul. It turns me into a different person. I hunger for the spirit of God to possess my soul. I want to join the band of prophets who create joyful noise even within earshot of their enemies and other squelchers of the Spirit. It can happen. It happens all the time. The testimonies are all around us if we listen.

I remember the story of a woman named Catherine who had a longing for music. She played in jazz bands as a young adult in Iowa, and one night, she drove to Iowa State University to hear the Pat Metheny Group, then an up-and-coming jazz quartet who were soon to become a worldwide sensation. Seated about ten feet away from the band, she heard and saw and felt in her body the sounds of creativity and musicianship.

Catherine chatted with the band after the show, a young woman with a dream, and Metheny encouraged her to follow that dream and study at Berklee College of Music, where he briefly taught and where his brother Mike was on the faculty. She moved to Boston and began her studies, hearing great music in venues around the city. One night, the word got out that Lyle Mays, the keyboardist with Metheny's group, was playing in a small club. Recalling his performance at the concert in Iowa, she got in her car, drove out to the club, and took her seat. Years later, she remembers the concert with complete clarity:

> When the music began, I knew I was going to witness something beyond special, something otherworldly. We were all blown away that night, transported. When the music was finally over, I went up to talk to Lyle and tell him how profoundly the music had impacted me. When I shook his hand, he looked into my eyes, and we were suddenly both speechless, in that moment acknowledging that something had

happened that was so far beyond words that speaking would be an injustice to the music. So we just looked at each other for what must have been an entire minute, grinning, and then we both said, "Yeah" to each other, and I walked away. That night inspired me to keep going with my music, to keep finding the depth inside myself to learn and grow as a musician.

There are times when writing about music feels awkward. The right words are elusive at best and can feel contrived at worst, particularly in the case of instrumental music that resonates within the soul. Yet there are still markers of transformation, and when I've taught jazz appreciation to university students, my assignments include writing about jazz concerts, describing what is happening among the musicians, and sharing how it impacts the writer and others. I advise avoiding the use of adjectives to get to the essence when listening to improvised music. The assignment encourages students to listen deeply, not only to the music but also to what they hear within themselves. What is brought back from these assignments is a new appreciation—if not an understanding, for who can really understand it?—of how the gift of music affects us, shapes us, and transforms us. And music might turn us into different people.

MOVING BEYOND THE AUDITORIUM

"The room came alive" is how my mother described the Louis Armstrong concert she attended two days after her nineteenth birthday. Every time I've pressed her for descriptions, she falters because she remembers a night that exceeded the limits of language. She did not have the words to describe the performance.

Her experience is even more remarkable considering the larger context of that concert. It was March 1955, less than one year after the US Supreme Court's decision in *Brown v. Board of Education* (1954) and just prior to the murder of Emmett Till (1955) and the Montgomery bus boycott (1955–56), three seminal events that sparked the American civil rights movement. Oil City, Pennsylvania, a town with a population of about eighteen thousand at the time, located in a corridor west of the Allegheny Mountains populated primarily by people of Scots-Irish descent, was hardly a community of racial diversity. A visit by a world-famous musician of such high caliber would have been a rare event here, let alone an African American performer at center stage with an integrated band.

One of the only reasons my mother got to see Armstrong at all is that Oil City served as a stopover between larger venues along his tour (hence the Thursday-night showtime). Ricky Riccardi, Armstrong's archivist, notes that the idea for the concert came about during a barnstorming season for Louis's All-Stars. No full itinerary of that week exists, but Riccardi reports that the concert took place during a series of one-nighters somewhere between the Crystal Ballroom in Michigan and State College, Pennsylvania. The band was soaring on the success of *Louis Armstrong Plays W. C. Handy*, the best-performing record of this season in Armstrong's career. Yet, despite the international reputation of the band, it is likely that Louis Armstrong, one of the greatest luminaries of American popular music and a pioneer of the jazz tradition, would not have been permitted to spend the night in a hotel owned by white folks in northwestern Pennsylvania.

It is also likely that Armstrong sang one of his signature songs of the tour, "Black and Blue"—a ballad composed by Thomas "Fats" Waller, with its final lyric musing about the color of his skin, "What did I do, to be so black and blue?" Not one to rush into a happier song, Armstrong would have likely paused to let the lyrics sink in. With that, my mother encountered a truth within the music that would continue to grow throughout her adult life into a concern for justice and inclusion.

Some might describe music, reductively, as sound vibrations through air, but music has the power to transform the room. And it's not just the listeners who are changed. The musicians are also profoundly affected. Saxophonist and jazz master David Liebman describes it this way:

> When you're playing and you're in control—there are moments when that actually happens—with good people, good audience, good sound, you are so present, so in control of the moment, it is the greatest high

and greatest feeling in the world. It is beyond anything. It is spiritual, it is physical, it is mental. It is vibe, it is groove. It's the whole deal. And that's what we go for every night when we play. Of course, you might only reach it a few times in your life. But that's worth the trip.

The French have a phrase to describe the experience: *le roi du monde.* King of the World. It is a natural high beyond anything I've ever known.

Compare this to the vocabulary used to describe moments of spiritual transcendence. Writers describe the sensation of being "lifted" or "free." Insight bursts into one's consciousness, and the invitation is given to step more deeply into life.

Many musicians speak of those transcendent moments and experiences as being formative to their vocations. Before he was a celebrated musician, back when Bobby McFerrin was a college student, he took a date to hear Miles Davis perform at a jazz club in Hollywood. It was the winter of 1971, and he and his girlfriend were standing in a long line that held little promise they would get tickets or find a way in. Then they saw a woman exiting the door of the club. She walked right up to them, announced, "I have two tickets that I'm not using," and handed them the tickets. Bobby had no idea who she was.

The two discovered that their seats were right next to the bandstand, right behind the piano with a clear view. It was an all-star ensemble, as all of Davis's bands were. As McFerrin puts it, "I walked out of that club that night molecularly changed."

I had never in my life heard music like that . . . I didn't really know what to do. I mean, my whole musical life and concept of music was altered that very moment.

You ever have moments like that in your life where something just changes you forever and you know you'll never be able to see yourself as a musician the same way again? Where everything is changed? Anyway, it was just one of those moments in my life that changed me forever . . . I walked out of the club thinking, "What was that? What was that?!"

It was just mind-blowing because I was a twenty-one-year-old composition student in college, and I was used to writing everything out, even writing out some solos that I wanted musicians to play—into controlling the music. Now here were these musicians letting the music control them, and I really saw that for the first time. And that changed my life.

Momentary epiphanies, soul-stirring as they may be, always point beyond themselves. They are signature experiences that point us toward daily living as well as to vocational calling. I consider them holy invitations toward deeper and wider expressions of how we live.

SIDEWALK REVELATION

There's a street sign in Louisville, Kentucky—the only one I've ever heard of—marking a moment of epiphany. Many years ago, I was walking up 4th Street in Louisville to meet a friend for dinner. I passed the Seelbach Hotel, where jazz groups have played regularly through the years, and crossed Muhammad Ali Boulevard. On the street corner, I saw a historical marker honoring a moment in Thomas Merton's life. The famed Trappist monk wrote about the integration of the hungers and hopes of human life. One side of the sign offered a very brief biography. The other side marked that singular moment in his life.

> A REVELATION—Merton had a sudden insight at this corner, March 19, 1958, that led him to redefine his monastic identity with greater involvement in social justice issues. He was "suddenly overwhelmed with the realization that I loved all these people. . . ." He found them "walking around shining like the sun."

Would that there were more street signs marking the location of a "sudden insight." Especially an epiphany of overflowing love that pushed someone deeper into social justice.

As I learned more about Merton's revelation, I also learned he was a serious jazz fan. In his monastic hermitage at the Abbey of Gethsemani, he listened to recordings of Mary Lou Williams, Django Reinhardt, and John Coltrane. When he traveled to Louisville for medical appointments, about an hour from the monastery, he would stick around to listen to jazz at a club on Washington Street. This monk who loved jazz offered in his writings a way to perceive these ecstatic, life-giving moments that awaken us to greater awareness and wider expressions of love and justice. In the opening pages of his well-known book *New Seeds for Contemplation*, he blows the moon dust off such experiences and puts them under a large spiritual umbrella that he names *contemplation*. As Merton explains, contemplation is

> life itself, fully awake, fully active, fully aware that it is alive. It is spiritual wonder. It is spontaneous awe at the sacredness of life, of being. It is gratitude for life, for awareness, and for being. It is a vivid realization of the fact that life and being in us proceed from an invisible, transcendent, and infinitely abundant Source.
>
> Contemplation is, above all, awareness of the reality of that Source.

What is contemplation? Consider the street signs that could be erected:

TRANSFORMATION—In the Latonia Theater on a Thursday night, Betsy heard Louis Armstrong, and it sent her on a continuing journey of change.

AWAKENING—On this mountain, the Mount of Transfiguration, the apostles Peter, James, and John experienced living fire.

PASSION—In this Oakland nightclub, Geoffrey's heart was opened by the surging power of McCoy's imagination.

INDESCRIBABLE—Just offstage in Boston, Catherine and Lyle shook hands, locked eyes, and could not find the words to say what they had experienced.

CHANGE—Here on the road to Gibeath-elohim, Saul met a band of frenzied prophets whose music turned him into a "different person."

REVEALED—In the illusory city of Hollywood, Bobby encountered Reality as he watched and listened to Miles Davis perform.

Each of the moments listed above points beyond itself. Each moment intersects heaven and earth, smashes through the limits of time, and moves life in new directions. Something happened. Something can always happen. Whatever it is, that *something* has the potential to bring us completely alive.

IMPROVISATION: EBO'S WALTZ

Grandma Ebo slipped the plain brown bag to me, saying,
"Wait until you get down the driveway
To open this." Despite my juvenile impatience,
I obeyed for once. And dismay arose when
I looked inside. Two musty Columbia LPs
Featured a pianist from distant Connecticut.
"That's Dave Brubeck,"
My mother exclaimed, as if a thirteen-year-old
Should revere the name.

One platter was warmly inviting,
With Mickey and Pluto on the cover and
The childish title, *Dave Digs Disney*.
Each tune gave a little whistle
Until the *tour de force* knocked me on my tail.
The sappiest of tunes, warbled by the cartoon maiden,
Suddenly thrust me into three different time signatures.
This was Dave's bag, said the notes,
And I had never heard someone enjoy music
Enough to create it.

Later I had that cardboard sleeve autographed:
"To Ebo, from Dave."
My new famous friend Brubeck smirked at the story,
For he had heard it before.
Ten million people had been infected long before me.
But I testify to the tune-spinning that crept through
The window of imagination.
And with thanks for my grandmother's gift,
I composed a waltz for her
that almost stays three beats to the measure.

She, in turn, bequeathed the signed record back to me,
Noting simply, "The music belongs to you."

I beg to differ.

CHAPTER TWO

WHAT ARE THEY DOING?

An Introduction to Jazz

Jazz, pfft! They just make it up as they go along.

—*Homer Simpson*

One evening, John Coltrane brought his quartet to Binghamton, New York. As my friend and fellow jazz musician Al Hamme relays the story, the venue was a pub called Gentleman Joe's, located in a rough section of town. Al and a friend got there early enough to claim seats next to the stage. As a saxophonist in his early twenties, Al was curious about Coltrane, who had played with Miles Davis, Dizzy Gillespie, and Thelonious Monk and was now making an international name for himself.

The quartet took the stage, and Al's companion nodded toward the pianist, Bobby Timmons, filling in for Coltrane's regular pianist, McCoy Tyner. Timmons had been friends with Coltrane from his Philadelphia days. Bobby was an outstanding pianist in his own right. Smartly dressed, he flashed a broad smile toward Al and the others nearby as he took a seat on the piano bench. Coltrane counted off the first tune, a medium-tempo blues, and Timmons held his own. After a flurry of saxophone notes, Bobby leaned in to play a hard-swinging piano solo. The patrons in the club nodded in rhythm and clapped loudly when his solo ended.

Pretty soon, however, the music began to change. Coltrane's band had begun to experiment with harmony in recent months. With the ferocious drumming of Elvin Jones thundering in circular rhythms and swirls of cymbals, and Jimmy Garrison's single-note bass lines accented heavily in repetitive pulses, Coltrane fired a fusillade of notes on his soprano sax.

The sounds intensified, and the pianist stopped playing. His hands sat motionless on the keyboard, and his jaw dropped open. With an astonished look, he swiveled toward my friend Al and asked, "What are they doing?"

Indeed. What are they doing?

This is a question worthy of anyone who listens to jazz. The music is alive and free, never static or fixed. It is a common experience for a fan to hear a recording, enjoy it, and lay down good money for a live concert. To their surprise, if the familiar song they love is played at all, it doesn't sound anything like the recording. There are exceptions, of course. For instance, a slickly produced, electronically synthesized ensemble playing mood music for lovers at an overpriced "jazz and music" festival may sound like a near replica of the album. But what about the hardcore bebop, the freewheeling, crazy-note music that has typified the jazz tradition? The variations between a recorded version and a live rendition could cause anyone to wonder, "What are they doing?"

The short answer is they are creating the music as they play.

One music writer once noted, "Jazz is a music in which the line between composition and performance is blurred, for its essence is improvisation: composing while performing." There may be a melody and a sequence of chord symbols on paper, but little of the music is actually written down. Even less is nailed down. This often bewilders classically trained musicians, who are usually bound to the black dots on a manuscript. Most jazz musicians are excellent readers of printed music since their craft requires performing in a wide variety of settings. Yet for them, music is *made*, not written.

Jazz reveals the truth that *written music* is a contradiction in terms. Music only exists in the air.

***

So what are they doing? Interpretation, first of all, with a personal spin.

For the first jazz musicians, music was learned by listening. They repeated what they heard and reinterpreted it. The earliest musicians were those who learned folk tunes, hymns, and dance songs and added a bit of bounce. It was more about entertainment than accuracy, about enlivening a melody, enriching its harmony, and providing danceable rhythms.

Jazz musicians invent and interpret as the genre continues to evolve. Since its beginnings in the early 1900s, new reinterpretations tend to bubble up every ten or fifteen years. Traditional jazz made way for syncopated popular songs. Swing music was answered by bebop. "West Coast" jazz softened the fury of bop, and hard bop ignited a new fire as the civil rights struggle in America welcomed cries for freedom and justice. The bossa nova craze flew in from Rio de Janeiro, while symphony conductors welcomed improvisers to join them onstage. As musicians plugged into amplifiers, the resulting electronic fusion rocked the music's foundations. And just as this splintered music was poised to spin into chaos, pianist Keith Jarrett sat down in concert halls in Europe and Japan to create ninety minutes of spontaneously created music. It's all jazz, ever surging forward. The whole kit and caboodle. The invention lies at the heart of it all, and the tradition refuses to cease reinventing itself. It is alive.

The paragon of this reinvention process was trumpeter Miles Davis, whose music never remained in one place for long. Like Coltrane, Davis's style never stopped changing, nor did it fail to confound band members and audiences. In his signature raspy whisper, he told one of his best quintets, "I pay you guys to practice on the bandstand." His advice to younger players was "Don't play what's there; play what's not there." And once, leaning over a young Herbie

Hancock on piano, he said, "Don't play the butter notes," leaving a bewildered young genius to try to figure out what that meant.

With cryptic one-liners like these, meant to offer direction, Davis sculpted the sounds of his extraordinarily talented bands. His lineups were constantly changing, and those who enjoyed his well-known recordings never heard the tunes performed the same way live as they remembered it.

"I have to change," Davis said repeatedly. "It's like a curse."

***

On a Sunday evening some years ago, a group of clergy joined me for a late show at Preservation Hall, the notable home of traditional jazz in New Orleans. The crowd was boisterous, and the leader of the band came out to greet us.

"Sounds like you are already having a good time," the band leader exclaimed.

The audience cheered in affirmation.

"Bet you didn't make it to church this morning," he added.

The crowd laughed in response.

"Well, then," he said, "tonight we are going to take you to church."

With that, he counted off "Just a Closer Walk with Thee," the first of a dozen or so familiar hymns that the band laid on the audience. As the musicians concluded with "When the Saints Go Marching In," the crowd leaped off the seats, clapped, danced, whooped, stomped, and sang along. We had been raised from the dead.

As our group stumbled back to our rooms on South Rampart Street after midnight, one of our group declared she had never heard church music like that. But in fact, the jazz tradition has its roots in church music too.

In my blended career as a pastor and pianist, I have encountered curious questions from faith communities related to the jazz world, seeking some connection between the two. One night, my jazz quartet finished a concert, and my grandmother stood in line to say hello. Grandma lived near the concert venue and waited patiently for the audience to move along. Approaching the

piano, she picked up a single sheet of paper with musical nota-
tion, stared at it, and analyzed it curiously. When the crowd had
dispersed, she asked, "How did all of you play for seven minutes
on one sheet of paper?"

"Grandma," I replied, "they ask me the same question back home
in my church on Sunday mornings. I stand in worship, read four or
five verses of scripture—essentially one page of notes—and proceed
to talk for eighteen minutes."

Grandma's question reminded me of the hometown synagogue
crowd who had just heard Jesus speak with authority and spin something new out of material they thought they understood. He left
listeners scratching their heads, asking, "Where does he get all this
stuff?"

This is the spiritual power of jazz at work, drawing on the same set
of skills: interpretation and invention. The improviser assumes there
is more insight available than what has been written down. There
is a greater Wisdom that wishes to speak if we only give it a voice.
There is something fresh and alive yet to be heard. New melodies
are released into the air when imagination dances with integrity.

***

It's important to understand what jazz improvisation truly is—and
what it isn't. *Webster's Dictionary* holds that "to improvise is to compose, or simultaneously compose and perform, on the spur of the
moment and *without any preparation*." For jazz (and the spiritual
life), that's a flawed definition. Yes, to improvise music is, in a sense,
to compose on the spur of the moment. But improvisation never happens without preparation. No jazz player gets up in front of others and
pulls notes out of the air. Rather, they dig the notes from fertile soil.

Music-making of this caliber can only happen after years of
instrumental practice and theoretical preparation. That's what Paul
Berliner discovered when he spent over fifteen years studying the
phenomenon of jazz improvisation. An ethnomusicologist at Northwestern University, Berliner dwelt within the jazz cultures of New
York and Chicago. He transcribed recorded solos. He interviewed

scores of musicians. He analyzed their practice habits. The following is what he says about his discovery.

> The popular definitions of improvisation that emphasize only its spontaneous, intuitive nature—characterizing it as the "making of something out of nothing"—are astonishingly incomplete. This simplistic understanding of improvisation belies the discipline and experience on which improvisers depend, and it obscures the actual practices and processes that engage them.

> Improvisation depends, in fact, on thinkers having absorbed a broad base of musical knowledge, including myriad conventions that contribute to formulating ideas logically, cogently, and expressively. It is not surprising, therefore, that improvisers use metaphors of language in discussing their art form. The same complex mix of elements and processes coexists for improvisers as for skilled language practitioners; the learning, the absorption, and utilization of linguistic conventions conspire in the mind of the writer or speaker—or, in the case of jazz improvisation, the player—to create a living work.

A "living work" assumes the people creating it are alive. That they are breathing, thinking, and engaging all that is around them. This is how the earliest jazz musicians expressed themselves. They played around with the melodies of their tunes. They twisted and teased the notes, pausing to punctuate or pushing to engage more deeply. Long before they knew any formal system of music theory, they understood the "personality" of each song. This intuition freed them to become more playful or more serious, depending on the mood of the conversation that was unfolding in the moment.

Isn't this how we talk with one another? Living conversations are not scripted any more than music is confined to a page. Our conversations proceed as they unfold. We joke around. We suggest and infer. We bicker, banter, and pause. We pay attention and respond in ways that fit the moment. Most of all, we reveal what's going on beneath the surface.

It's no wonder that some jazz musicians regard improvisation as tale-spinning, like the description of the saxophone solos of the legendary Lester Young: "Every time he plays, he tells a story." His improvisations often took a narrative shape, stating a simple theme, developing it, and bringing it to its conclusion. When you listened to Young's improvisations, it was like you were hearing his commentary on the songs.

On occasion, a complete short story is spun. Musicians revere the historic moment when Paul Gonsalves played an extended hard-swinging solo at the 1956 Newport Jazz Festival so powerful that it reignited the lagging career of Duke Ellington.

Gonsalves stood to blow a saxophone solo on "Diminuendo and Crescendo in Blue" and proceeded to work up the late-night crowd into a frenzy. For six minutes and twenty-two seconds, he invented a sustained reflection on the blues. A woman in a cocktail dress got out of her box seat and began to dance. The aisles soon filled with jitterbuggers. Cheers came from the crowd and the orchestra, egging on Gonsalves. Fearing a riot, festival organizer George Wein stood offstage and shouted to Ellington, "That's enough! That's enough!" Duke ignored him, and Gonsalves dug in deeper. The crowd of seven thousand cheered. When the venue cleared out, many went home acknowledging they had just been part of history. The ensuing recording, *Ellington at Newport*, became Duke's best-selling album.

Musicians work hard to lift the music from the page (if there's a page) and release it into the air. It takes disciplined, technical preparation to play this music. It also requires the freedom to take enormous risks.

A WELL-INFORMED RISK

"Improvisation is an act of faith," pianist Jim McNeely said to me one night at the Deer Head Inn, a venerable jazz club in the Pocono Mountains of Pennsylvania.

Improvisation requires risk. The act of playing jazz—like daily life, like the spiritual life—is an informed risk. Improvisation happens through nimble fingers, serious training in music theory and form, and a willingness to jump into uncharted territory.

Fortunately, this risk and freedom come with a safety net of grace. If a musician hits a sour note or flubs a rhythm, it cannot be replayed, only forgiven. There will be another opportunity to play better notes on another day. This is a process in action I've seen a thousand times.

One night, I asked one of my daughters to join me for an evening at Blues Alley, a wonderful club in the Georgetown section of Washington, DC. We hopped aboard a bus near her university, paid the cover charges, ordered dinner and drinks, and waited for the show to begin.

The crowd on that Friday night was buzzing with excitement as the famed band The Yellowjackets took the stage. The drummer began an African rhythm, and the bass player quickly joined in. The pianist punctured the air with syncopated chords, playing in a fierce rhythm. The music was new to us, but we quickly discerned the melody as the saxophonist played it. The tune swirled and churned, building toward a climax.

Suddenly the band stopped, and the saxophonist leaped into the unknown. He played a flurry of notes by himself before the band entered with precision and surged forward. The whole performance became much more complicated. I would not have been surprised to hear someone at the next table ask the Bobby Timmons question "What are they doing?" The best reply would have been, "We don't know yet."

These moments of adventurous ambiguity can be disconcerting to those musicians and music lovers who prefer to have all their notes confined to a page. For them, the performance follows a script. It moves ahead as the composer wants it to unfold. The music is predictable, reveals few surprises, and always happens on cue. It will be judged later for accuracy and expertise. The critics may recognize that a small measure of interpretation can add personality to the performance—within the limitations of the written score—but overall, it's an evaluation of how well the musicians played the pre-arranged notes.

When jazz musicians take flight, nobody knows what will come next. Even the players! The saxophonist begins to compose in motion.

The pianist makes instantaneous decisions about supporting the sax, deciding if they will go where their colleague is leading. The bass player anchors the exploration with notes and patterns, but they and the drummer are also free to push the music toward more intensity. This could drive the saxophonist even further into the sky.

This is music in the making, the essence of jazz. Grace is offered in the face of enormous risks. If the song is evaluated too soon, all creativity will implode. If the cocreators stop listening to one another, the whole performance can disintegrate. If any one of the team members dominates or withholds their input, the enjoyment of true collaboration is lost.

At any moment, there is risk and potential. The tune could disintegrate into self-indulgent blathering. Or it could unlock fresh insights and lead us in new directions. When the experiment works, there are broad smiles on the musicians' faces and a thumping response from the audience. A sheer ecstasy in shared art.

What are they doing? Risking. Inventing. Having fun. Offering grace. Receiving gifts.

A NEW SONG

I was recently involved in a jazz vespers event in a church, during which one listener became enchanted as our bassist created a solo out of the hymn "Be Thou My Vision." Her mouth opened in astonishment as Tony deconstructed the familiar melody. She leaned forward in amazement as he built something fresh out of phrases of two or three notes. She was the first to cheer as he spun new gold out of straw. When the vespers was over, she sprinted forward to say, "You were singing a new song!"

I loved the comment because she was quoting one of my favorite Bible verses, "O sing to the Lord a new song." It was a remarkable moment. Traditional churchgoers don't always appreciate new songs; sadly, many of them cling only to the old ones. Yet the line appears repeatedly in the sacred text, including six times in the book of Psalms and twice in the book of Revelation.

My favorite setting of the verse appears in an astonishing poem from the prophet Isaiah. He hears music that is so full of life that the sea sings along, the desert rejoices, the mountains reverberate, and every human voice joins in. Even God cries out like a pregnant Mother:

> For a long time I have held my peace,
>   I have kept still and restrained myself;
> now I will cry out like a woman in labor.

A whole new creation is about to be born! And then the birthing Creator offers something more:

> I will lead the blind
>
>   by a road they do not know,
> by paths they have not known
>   I will guide them.
> I will turn the darkness before them into light,
>   the rough places into level ground.
> These are the things I will do,
>
>   and I will not forsake them.

In my mind, the best jazz musicians are not only those who merely express themselves or "cry out in labor." They are the ones who lead us down a road we would not have known in any other way.

In jazz, as well as in the spiritual life, more than expression, we want insight. We want to travel a road that takes us into the presence of the ultimate wow factor, God—a beautiful presence where there is light, levity, refreshment, and new life.

The freedom and grace of jazz might lead an observer to mistakenly believe that its practitioners somehow approach it with less reverence than traditional music. It is a well-documented fact, for example, that John Coltrane worked hard to develop his craft and practiced constantly. After his first big break with Dizzy Gillespie's band in the early 1950s, he took a job with the Miles Davis Quintet.

When Coltrane played with Davis's group, he improvised solos that could last fifteen or twenty minutes. It got to the point that it annoyed Miles, who, even as he nodded for Coltrane to take his turn at a solo, couldn't help but wince.

One night, Miles finally asked, "Trane, why do you play so long?"

The young saxophonist replied, "It took that long to get it all in."

Another time, after a lengthy Coltrane improvisation, Miles asked him, "Why do you play so many notes?"

John responded, "Once I get started, I don't know how to stop."

Miles had the solution: "Take the horn out of your mouth."

After Coltrane parted ways with Davis and started his own group, something changed. One morning, he told his wife about a vision that came to him. "I heard a song," he claimed. It sounded heavenly. He spent his remaining years searching for that song on his saxophone (more on this in chapter 3).

Needless to say, Coltrane used a lot of notes. There's even an apocryphal story about a music fan who, years later, asked him the same question Miles Davis used to ask: "Why do you play so many notes?"

Coltrane said, "I'm looking for the right note."

"What if you should find it?" the interviewer said.

Coltrane thought for a minute and said, "I'll play it again."

Within the improvisations of jazz, we often hear a yearning for the right note, the holy note, the healing note, the beautiful note.

***

Look at a piano keyboard, and you will see basically the same configuration as you would have seen in the early eighteenth century. Not much has changed about those black and white keys. There are no new notes. But there are near-infinite new configurations of the existing notes.

New songs are built from the scraps of old ones. New note configurations from earlier versions. Maybe that's what it means to "sing to the Lord a new song," as the prophetic text of Isaiah says. "If we listen to the singing, we discover that the new song is constituted by the same old words. The old words are recovered and reclaimed," commented scholar Walter Brueggemann about that song-text.

The new song is not a return to a kinder, gentler age. Neither is it a trip down Nostalgia Avenue. It is, rather, a radical discovery that the songs our mothers, our traditions, and our holy texts taught us to sing possess transformative, interpretive power and movement for a new day. The new song given by God is always a song that began in the past yet is brought forward to this time, this place, and these circumstances.

When musicians make jazz, they participate in an act of new creation. They take old songs and bring them forward into something new. They build new melodies with the basic materials of harmony, rhythm, and old tunes. They create on the spot with imagination, humor, and great freedom. Is the new song inspired? Is it a Holy Spirit moment? Perhaps. But like most acts of God, the inspiration revealed comes in subtlety and through hard work and flashes of unpredictable brilliance.

There is an old story about a famous trumpeter in which a woman asked him, "What is going on inside your head when you play jazz?"

"Lady," he replied, "if I could tell you, your brain would explode."

That's the risk of the new song—the freedom and the grace. What jazz affirms is the refusal to be confined, enshrined, or even defined. There is vitality at the heart of the new song, at the heart of this music. It risks everything to embrace freedom, and part of its new-song insistence is how jazz not only creates the new song but how it steps over boundaries, real or imaginary.

IMPROVISATION: TALE-SPINNING

Step into
The song,
hear it
unfold.
The invitation
beckons from
a future we
cannot know
until that
first step
begins.

There is
more joy
dancing with a
scrap of Melody,
leading,
following,
twirling tunefully
as you glide
across the floor.
Spin a tale

sideways by
embarking on a
journey that
others can join.

Call this a solo,
but it's a ballet
for all who have
ears to hear
and feet tapping
in the Groove.

CHAPTER THREE

CROSSING THE DOTTED LINE
Discerning Sacred and Secular

Jazz music was invented by demons for the torture of imbeciles.
—*Dr. Henry van Dyke*

The first time I ever played jazz piano in church was at a Sunday event when our teenage youth group presented a skit. The text chosen for the sermon was the famous parable of the prodigal son. An upstart youth demands from his father an advance on the inheritance. Receiving it without so much as a reprimand or a whimper, he heads into the city. There he squanders it on "loose living." That was my moment in the performance: a party scene in which I sat at an upright piano, a bowler hat on my head, with a few caricatures of "loose women" hanging on my shoulders. I banged out some New Orleans stride piano in the style of Jelly Roll Morton. The sonic inference was clear: jazz music, particularly of a Crescent City bent, was the soundtrack for "dissolute living."

On his way out the door, one man joked he had never heard that kind of music in church. His inference was that he never expected to hear it there again. For him, as for many, there is a clear line dividing "sacred" and "secular"—and I had crossed it. Music once performed in the waiting rooms of bordellos did not belong in a Protestant sanctuary, and the youth group's skit had reinforced this.

In my youthful exuberance, I didn't realize I was contributing to a long-time conflict in the church between notions of sacred and secular and where each belongs. In August 1921, Anne Shaw Faulkner published an article in *Ladies Home Journal*. Her title asked the question "Does Jazz Put the Sin in Syncopation?" On the cusp of the Roaring Twenties, Ms. Faulkner sounded the alarm on America's new popular music. Jazz incites human passions, she declared with Victorian earnestness and the assumption that untamed human passions are inherently ugly and unseemly. Faulkner quoted a letter from clergyman Henry Van Dyke, who gave his verdict on jazz:

> As I understand it, it is not music at all. It is merely an irritation of the nerves of hearing, a sensual teasing of the strings of physical passion. Its fault lies not in syncopation, for that is a legitimate device when sparingly used. But "jazz" is an unmitigated cacophony, a combination of disagreeable sounds in complicated discords, a willful ugliness and a deliberate vulgarity.

It is unfortunate that Van Dyke, an otherwise cultured Presbyterian minister and professor at Princeton University, rendered such a statement and carried it into the church.

Now shift with me toward sacred space. There is a Christian congregation in San Francisco that affirms the great spiritual potential of jazz. The namesake of Saint John's African Orthodox Church is none other than Saint John Coltrane. It is the only church in the world named after a jazz musician. And the people of that congregation view Trane's music as an entrance to the holy.

Is there some deeper spiritual power at work? What constitutes sacred? Sometimes it's the jazz musicians who offer new understandings.

***

Some musicians look to classical music by the masters to declare what is sacred—Johann Sebastian Bach, for instance. Bach worked in churches and produced a prolific pile of music deemed sacred. Some of it provided musical settings of biblical and theological texts, and some is purely instrumental music. Bach expanded on existing hymn tunes, but let's be honest: a fugue is a fugue. Beautiful, of course, and built with logical precision. Without a reference point, a fugue is merely a sequence of notes, just like any other tune.

Bach regularly inscribed his works with the dedication *Soli Deo Gloria* ("Glory to God alone"). This was his reference point, his personal affirmation from the heart. If others did not share his perspective, they still heard a gorgeous melody enriched by ingenious counterpoint. The music stood on its own virtues for a culture that understood the language of music. If, however, average listeners hear a masterwork in a musical language they do not understand, they could dismiss it as a tune with too many notes.

But what if *sacred* simply refers to events and experiences when God is present? Nothing more and certainly nothing less. Not necessarily confined to specific spaces. Not divided between church and street or street and jazz club.

None of us can create the moment in which the sacred enters. We can only receive it, dare to name it, and pray for it to happen again and again. When people experience God within tone and rhythm, that is sacred.

To perceive music, especially jazz, as sacred or holy involves paying attention to it. We are invited to remain open to the surprise of a spiritual presence. Traditional religions and their sacred texts understand this. But sometimes the followers of those texts miss it.

Many Christians, even as they revere the Bible, fail to understand what the scriptures offer and explore. The Bible gives field reports of God's presence and activity. Something happens—the sea splits open, an unanticipated healing happens, an unexpected child is born, a hungry crowd is fed, a dead person returns to life—and somebody is there to experience the moment. Maybe it was confusing at first, even cacophonous, but something profound was made in these moments. And somebody saw it, heard it, and wrote it down.

The sacred moment is the God moment. It may enliven, confront, generate awe, unleash pathos, or call people to a new purpose for their lives. This is what a house of worship like Saint John's African Orthodox Church in San Francisco affirms. Because of the God they hear speaking in their music, they have created a soup kitchen, given a hand-up to the homeless, provided space for addiction recovery groups, and led antiracism training events. Dare we call these activities *secular*? What gives us the authority to create false dichotomies dictating where God can and cannot be present?

What if God inhabits music the same way memory inhabits a sweet aroma? We smell cinnamon and are transported back to Grandma's kitchen. Similarly, we can hear a tune, even a secular one, and be carried into heaven or directed more deeply toward earth. St. John's identifies the significance of music as an act of worship. It is a gift of God and to be welcomed as such. It is a gift with holy potential. And that worship, that music, that God changes us.

Perhaps we could all do with a little more music in our spiritual lives. After all, church folks can have the tendency to overdose on words. Spoken liturgies. Homilies. Spoken prayers. A joke I once heard suffices to give the picture: A church organist was conversing with the preacher one day. The preacher said, "There is a moment in our worship service when I will move from the pulpit to the communion table. Could you cover it with a soft tune?" "No problem, Rev," says the organist. "In fact, there's a moment when I must move from the organ console to the piano bench. Would you mind mumbling a few words?"

The term *secular* signifies not the absence of God but indifference to God, which is where many of us find ourselves at least some of the time. If *sacred*, on the other hand, means that God is present, or at least potentially available, there is almost nothing that is secular.

The jazz-inspired spiritual life invites us to move from indifference to awareness, from randomness to rhythm, where the Holy might surprise us and redirect our lives.

WAKING UP TO THE SACRED

A musical colleague tells of a signature moment that he described as "waking up from a bad dream." A highly regarded jazz pianist and college professor, he was attending a national jazz education conference at the time.

"I was riding in an elevator," he says, "probably headed back down to the bar to get tanked up again." The elevator door opened, and vocalist Bobby McFerrin stepped into the elevator.

"He took a long look into my eyes," he said, "saw my wrecked state, and moaned, 'Ohh, ohh.' McFerrin teared up, caught his breath, and got off on the next floor. He didn't say anything more. He knew. I knew. I was living without God, and it was damaging me." This experience was a wake-up call.

One of the most dramatic awakenings in the jazz community as a whole happened in the early days of the career of John Coltrane. With Coltrane on sax, the Miles Davis Quartet quickly became one of the foremost jazz bands in the country. It was also riddled with addiction, sometimes referred to as the D and D Band, short for "drug and drink." Coltrane fell into a deep heroin addiction. It damaged his work so badly that Miles fired him.

Ashamed, Coltrane returned to his house in Philadelphia and locked himself in an upstairs room. Accounts of what happened next differ, but Trane emerged drug-free after a week of cold turkey. He would later describe that experience as an awakening to the presence of God and a return to what he called "the right path." Here's how he described it:

> During the year 1957, I experienced, by the grace of God, a spiritual awakening which was to lead me to a richer, fuller, more productive life. At that time, in gratitude, I humbly asked to be given the means and privilege to make others happy through music. I feel this has been granted through His grace. ALL PRAISE TO GOD.

Both Trane and his music were transformed. The sloppy eighth notes from his final recordings with Miles Davis were sharpened. His music surged with fresh power and clarity. Davis hired him again, at least for a while, but Trane was accelerating toward the angels. Practicing ceaselessly with the same intensity that he once gave to feeding his addiction, he recorded an astounding album called *Blue Train*. Every tune surged as a force of nature. It was followed by the album *Giant Steps*, a nod to the complex harmonies of his new compositions and an affirmation of the movement in his life.

And then Coltrane kept going, creating tunes with simpler structures but no less power. Moving from the pinnacle of human achievement to the full incorporation of divine grace, he began to title his songs "The Father, the Son and Holy Ghost," "Ascension," and "Dear Lord," as well as creating suites like "A Love Supreme" and "Meditations." Coltrane made a move beyond pure human effort and excellence to an acknowledgment of the divine love that surrounds us.

Sacred and *secular* are terms used to create narrow views of where God can or cannot act, even as the Lord God declared to the prophet Isaiah, "Heaven is my throne, and the earth is my footstool." An eternal God does not hide in a temple or hymnal or designated spaces. There is more sacred music to discover when our parsing stops and God comes in.

"God made one world, not two," said jazz bassist John Patitucci. "We don't live in a Christian world some of the time and a secular world the rest of the time."

One world or two? Jesus of Nazareth spoke of only one world. He knew the scriptures. As a well-schooled Jew, he knew Israel had a "code" for holiness, kept in the scroll of Leviticus. He knew that *sacred* was considered what was kept within temple walls or what was held as sacred by gatekeepers. Yet he stepped over those boundaries to heal lepers, touch corpses, converse with outsiders, and spend time with those shunned by a code of morality. As Jesus spoke, healed, and communed with others, he taught that it is far more life-giving to live simply and generously, looking for God's presence in all things, bringing God's presence to all beings.

One world, infused with life, surging with the syncopations of the Spirit.

***

Many may dismiss Bobby McFerrin as the guy who sang "Don't Worry, Be Happy," an infectious ditty that still lingers on the airwaves. What these critics don't know is that he invented that song in the studio after serious reflection on the Sermon on the Mount. He sang all the parts and scored a number one hit in the process. When he hit it big, he shrugged off the "star machine" of American idolatry, singing only where and when he sensed it could make a positive difference.

As McFerrin developed solo concerts (McFerrin, a microphone, and nothing else), he would pull people out of their auditorium seats mid-show and bring them on stage. Spontaneously, he would sing a short musical phrase, repeat it, and motion for them to sing it too. When they did, he sang something over it, then motioned to another group to sing that while he improvised yet a third melody over it all.

Imagine 150 people in a circle three or four deep, arranged by vocal parts, all singing improvisational, spontaneous songs like this. That was the essence of a weeklong retreat on the Hudson River that I attended where McFerrin gathers a crowd annually for "circle singing," an imaginative exercise of spontaneously creating songs in four-part harmony. The event was held at the Omega Center, a former Jewish summer camp, now a year-round facility for the yoga and health-food crowd. We sang wordless vocals mostly, lingering for eight or ten minutes. By the end of the first evening's three-hour singing session, my cup was full. Really full. It was a deeply spiritual experience of the power of music.

Bobby brought an all-star faculty of four other vocalists with him. We spent time together, splitting into smaller groups. There were all kinds of people there—music teachers, vocalists, a smattering of conventional religious people like me, and a substantial number of folks who had been harmed or victimized by some form of religion. That was fascinating. When we sang together, all of us reached above the differences. The songs consisted of sounds and syllables sung with deep passion, filled with intoxicating rhythm— and healing.

Returning to my cabin one night, I reflected in my journal:

This is a nonsectarian bunch,
but they know the power unleashed in music-making.
The songs swell and rise;
a hundred and fifty tongues are loosed,
three hundred feet are moving.
Every heart strangely moved, a few budged.
Smiles radiate the room,
while the Spirit inhabits the tones and rhythms.
Even if She is unnamed by many, Spirit is here
with Bright Wings fluttering.

At the very conclusion of the gathering, a group member offered a big hug. She said, "I know you're a minister, and I'm an atheist. I have to say, this is the most spiritual event I have ever known. When we sing, it's all about love—a love greater and more inviting than anything I have ever known. It fills us, and we reach beyond everything else to take and share it."

No insult intended, but those don't sound like the words of an atheist. She perceived a Great Love at the heart of that music-making. And she honored it by refusing to diminish it.

As for me, I have rarely known such euphoria, which lingered and healed me so deeply. All my worries evaporated when we sang together. Body, soul, and spirit were united as we swayed to rhythms, reached for fresh harmony, and blended with that creative company in a new song. The experience was fostered by the maestro's mysticism. A quiet man, Bobby McFerrin told me as we walked together one afternoon that he had considered the monastic life as a teenager. "I wanted nothing more than to pray, be quiet, and reflect on scripture," he said.

Suddenly, he stopped on the path, turned to look me in the eye, and asked, "Preacher Bill, what is your favorite book of the Bible? I mean, other than the Psalms."

As we talked about scripture, he said he was working on the Gospel of Matthew an inch at a time, memorizing the verses that resonated with his soul. It was a deep moment where words met music and Spirit.

CAN GOD FIND US THROUGH MUSIC?

I often ask fellow musicians, "How has God found you through music?" The answers are so varied and powerful that it wouldn't surprise me if some future mystic discerns that the Holy Spirit plays the trombone.

What about you? Have you encountered a moment in which you were caught up in something *big*? Something *alive*?

All of us have had liminal moments when any dividing line evaporates. At the surly age of seventeen, I bolted myself in my bedroom after our family's Thanksgiving meal, unsocial, grouchy. No doubt they were glad to see me retreat. Turning on the stereo and plugging in my headphones, I stretched out on my bed to listen to a newly acquired Keith Jarrett album. *Arbor Zena* features Keith on piano, Charlie Haden on bass, and the Norwegian saxophonist Jan Garbarek improvising over the shimmering light of a chamber orchestra.

The music punctured my mood. It was the first of many of my own wow moments. I felt—quite literally—lifted into the air, high into the clouds, free from all adolescent burdens. Had I eaten too much turkey? Too much pumpkin pie? Was it a moment explained by, as Ebenezer Scrooge tried to dismiss Marley's ghost, "You may be an undigested bit of beef, a blot of mustard, a crumb of cheese, a fragment of an underdone potato"? I cannot say. It was the first of many liminal moments, often beyond words, where jazz became the conduit for the Spirit, and I was transformed, if only for a brief time. And I constantly hear stories from others who have had similar experiences.

One of our church's wandering children returned one year for Christmas Eve. Sally began her spiritual journey as a Presbyterian, fell in love with Quaker silence, went Buddhist, and may now list herself as "none of the above." She came to the 9:00 p.m. service to hear her mother sing with the choir, then stuck around for the annual 11:00 p.m. jazz service that we have been doing for over twenty years. At the end of the service, the jazz band broke into a salsa version of "Joy to the World." Dancing broke out in the aisles.

After the service finally wound down, she found me. Her face looked stunned; her voice was inarticulate. She tried to speak, then paused. Finally, she stammered out, "The Holy is here. It is palpable."

"Now, Sally," I said with a twinkle in my eye, "all we were doing was syncopating some Christmas carols." She started to laugh, a great big Santa laugh, and slowly wandered back out into the world.

Christmas seems to be a time when the veil between *sacred* and *secular* is particularly thin. A few Christmas Eves ago, I stood to preach and was struck by the fact that this is the very nature of the Christian story. God becomes a human child. The Ineffable Spirit takes on human flesh. The Creator sets aside all power, sheds heavenly privilege, and becomes part of the Creation. The sacred kisses the secular. God is with us—that's the heart of it all. As the brilliant theologian Dietrich Bonhoeffer summarized the mystery:

> Christ took upon himself this human form of ours. . . . In the Incarnation the whole human race recovers the dignity of the image of God. . . . Through fellowship and communion with the incarnate Lord, we recover our true humanity . . . [we] retrieve our solidarity with the whole human race. By being partakers of Christ incarnate, we are partakers in the whole humanity which he bore.

The truth of this comes from familiar words from the Gospel of John that ground us all year long: "What has come into being in him was life, and the life was the light of all people."

Light and life. These are the universal gifts of God. We don't have to work for them. They are already present with us, ready to be received. God dignified human life on the day that Jesus was born, a sign of God's longing for heaven and earth to be united and all of life to be integrated.

For me, that is music to my ears. Any music that dignifies human life and voices human passion belongs to God. Jazz belongs to God.

"The earth is the Lord's, and the fullness thereof," Psalm 24 rings out. If there is a line between "sacred" and "secular," it is a dotted line.

Daily life is the only spiritual life we have. The work of our hands, just like the work of our imaginations, is what we offer to God—to praise God, pray, and pursue God's ways.

IMPROVISATION: MIND THE GAP

Surely the Lord is in this place—and I did not know it!
—*Genesis 28:17*

Stepping toward the train in Glasgow
she tugged on my sleeve and pointed:
MIND THE GAP
was the Scots' warning.
They could not protect us
from the empty space
between train and track.
The warning heeded,
saved from certain doom
or at least an entrapped shoe,
I mull over other gaps,
especially that space between
heaven and earth.

If we pad around on
the Holy One's footstool,
is there any place here
free from an act of God?
Could Jesus blow bebop

in that trumpet's crazy notes?
If the deep chord consoles
or dissonance awakens,
can music be easily dismissed?

Sound, sanctified,
seeps into the gap,
transgressing arrogance,
smashing defended borders,
empowering availability.
Perhaps the gap is pregnant space.
Or perhaps it doesn't really exist,
An illusion for avoidance.

CHAPTER FOUR

A MESSAGE FROM HEADQUARTERS

Now that I think about it, it really depends on whether a player conceives of "nothing" as the lack of "something," or pregnant with "everything."

—*Keith Jarrett*

In 1987, Dave Brubeck got off the phone and shook his head in disbelief. He had just declined an invitation to write music for the first papal mass in the United States.

The call came from the diocesan offices in San Francisco, asking him to write a prelude based on a text from the Gospel of Matthew, from which the Roman Catholic Church finds its support for the papacy: "Upon this rock, I will build my church. The gates of hell shall not prevail against it."

Brubeck declared himself unworthy of creating this piece of music meant to proclaim that gospel text, a piece that would premier at Candlestick Park in San Francisco. "I can't do that," Dave thought. But that night, he went to bed and dreamed the entire piece. When he woke, he asked his conductor to call back and see if he could reconsider the invitation. "I think I received a message from headquarters," he added.

Brubeck went on to compose a nine-minute chorale and fugue, timed sufficiently to accompany the Popemobile as it entered through the center field fence and circled the stadium for pontifical waving. The work would begin with a brass fanfare of seventy horns with a percussion section. A massive choir would sing a gorgeous chorale that explicated the theme. After another fanfare of brass, the choir would sing a complicated fugue in C minor built on the musical theme of the chorale.

Seventy-two thousand people would attend the papal mass. Seven hundred singers volunteered to rehearse the piece and sing in the choir. A large orchestra had been employed to play in support of the anthem. The Dave Brubeck Quartet was expected to join the performance with a special improvisational section Dave included in the score.

Except the quartet never joined in. Before the performance, a church dignitary looked over the shoulder of the conductor and discovered the improvisational portion in the score. He directed the conductor to go ahead with the chorale and fugue but yanked the jazz section out of the piece. When asked why, he responded, "Because there can't be improvisation at a papal mass. The press would have a field day."

Dave shook his head again. And when the moment came, the jazz musicians listened to the choir and orchestra perform Brubeck's composition from a distance.

Dave, though, would later say he received his vindication. At one point in the mass, Pope John Paul II stepped to the brink of the platform, looked down at Dave, and made the sign of the cross. Dave said to Russell Gloyd, his conductor, "Did he just bless us?"

Russell replied, "Either that, or he's trying to learn to conduct in 4/4."

I love this story not only for its humor but for what it reveals. It is striking that a jazz luminary like Brubeck would have the same self-doubts as any other mere mortal. Despite his accomplishments, Dave maintained a measured perspective on his own abilities. It's also striking, but less surprising, that a church official was anxious about going off script—by a song that flew off the page and into the heart and spirit.

Most of all, the story reveals the tension between divine creativity and human control.

***

For Dave Brubeck to claim he received "a message from headquarters" pointed to his understanding of a God who is the source of all things, including his nine-minute chorale and fugue. Brubeck did not say the musical piece was dictated from above but that he discerned and received it from below. It came to him inspired, unexpected, and readily welcomed.

This opens us to the mystery of divine creativity, what some artists and musicians name the *muse*. By speaking this way, they welcome the gift of a new insight or a fresh piece of creative work while honoring the mystery of its Source.

It's this understanding of the Source that the Hebrew scripture affirms through its opening song in Genesis—in a litany of abundance. The song begins, "When God began to create the heavens and the earth" and follows a progression of days, repeated refrains ("it was evening, it was morning") followed by a repeated blessing: "It was good." After six days of subdividing eternity, God freely took time to pause, breathe, and make room for the creation to breathe on its own. Thus, the first biblical week begins as a very fine song.

The song doesn't conclude there, though. After the day-seven pause, the song continues into day eight and beyond. The song goes on, carrying the blessed command, "Be fruitful and multiply!" Thus, God builds generativity into the initial creation. We see evidence in that new robin's nest in our weeping cherry tree. We hear it in the trombonist who stands to improvise a new melody. New life is still under construction, always emerging.

The message from headquarters keeps singing. It is not finished. Theologian Ann Pederson says it is tempting to think, like Aristotle, that once the world is made, everything is fixed and classified, that the world is established and stays that way. Pederson compares this sense to the classical composer who writes a symphony. All the black dots are fixed on paper, right where they need to be, never to be changed.

But contemporary physics suggests something different. This is not how the world functions. Creation is more like jazz. Dr. Pederson compares God to a jazz musician, able to create something out of nothing so it can live and breathe and grow and change. The primary characteristic of creation is not that of dots fixed on paper but all that is *alive in dynamic form*. Creation has a past: all things were created. But creation has a present tense: the world is alive, changing, evolving, singing.

"In the beginning God," the first four words of the King James Bible, are the words Duke Ellington used to govern the theme of his music when he was commissioned to compose and perform his first concert of sacred jazz in 1965. Six syllables, an incomplete sentence recurring through the set. Exactly.

Unfinished. It was merely the beginning.

But there is an opposite and equal temptation toward control. I hear it in those who speak of creation only in the past tense, as if everything is already settled and categorized. In my own spiritual tradition as a Presbyterian Christian, we have a Book of Order. My people come from uptight Scots who nailed everything down with hard, rational nails. Predictability provides great comfort to many in my tribe, which in part explains why there has never been jazz improvisation at a papal mass.

What is alive is alive. As theologians David F. Ford and Daniel W. Hardy observe, there is an irrepressible quality to God's ongoing creation. They call it "the jazz factor." The Bible portrays a God who is so completely alive that creativity constantly bubbles up, and the life of Jesus continues to show that jazz factor.

In the Gospel of John, an insightful story reveals Jesus healing a paralyzed person by the miracle pool of Beth-zatha. Ignoring all the popular customs surrounding the pool, the Healer heals a man on the Sabbath—against prevailing custom, on the day of the week when healing was forbidden. When the religious rule-keepers decry his work, Jesus counters by saying, "My Father is still working, and so am I." They had their small acre of life categorized, labeled, and managed. Jesus did not stick to their script. For this, they were so enraged that they wanted to kill Jesus.

We love our scripts. They are tidy and predictable. Anxiety can be reduced if people know what to expect. At a recent worship conference, for example, I was invited to prepare a jazz vesper service. The coordinator requested all the materials in print to produce an order of worship for the participants and to distribute a complete script for the worship leaders. The finished script listed the exact timing of each component of the service, down to the minute. I smiled to myself, thinking, *And she has booked jazz musicians?*

I prayed the jazz musicians' prayer right before the service, "Creator of All, let something happen today that is not written down in the worship bulletin."

***

When imagination is suppressed, when order is imposed, when the jazz factor of God's creation is denied, the human need for control becomes addictive—and has led to some of the grimmest chapters in human history.

Writing about the political changes in Germany in the early 1930s, Canadian scholar and historian Michael Kater noted that the changes were reflected in the music. In the Roaring Twenties, Germany loved jazz. The toe-tapping music set spirits free from the deep poverty following World War I.

When Adolph Hitler came to power, jazz was mistrusted, questioned, and eliminated. With the faces of jazz being Benny Goodman, a Jew, and Louis Armstrong, whose dark skin contrasted that of the Aryan "master race" proposed by Nazi racial ideology, the Third Reich banned jazz from its stages and airwaves. It was too spontaneous, too unpredictable, too free. Hitler insisted on repetitive, simple, uniform marches that kept everyone in step. Creative artists who strayed outside of what the government deemed acceptable were jailed or put into concentration camps. That posse of authoritarians knew they could not keep a thumb on the masses if they had free-wheeling musicians on the streets.

History shows us this is what repressive governments do. They impose order in their people and predictability in their God. The issue is freedom. At such points in history, the music is codified, and the church is controlled. God is not free. Neither is anybody else. Creativity can be a threat to those who wish to maintain control.

LOVE AT THE HEART OF ALL THINGS

It is no wonder, then, that freewheeling jazz musicians often feel nervous when they step into societies that control the arts, or even when stepping into the precincts of organized religion. Jazz cannot be confined to marches (or worship bulletins).

The first time I invited a college classmate to play his bass for an outdoor church service and picnic, he was immediately suspicious. In his eyes, the singing was tolerable, the food was tasty, and the congregation's appreciation for his talent was effusive. What offended him was the pastor's talk to children during the worship service. "He's trying to indoctrinate those young souls," he exclaimed. "It's mind control!" When we met later to talk about it, he revealed his reaction to his own narrow religious upbringing, an experience that still evoked a vehement distrust of religion.

For those creative and sensitive souls who didn't meet the jazz factor in religious communities, this is a common reaction. After my friend lowered his temperature, I pointed out that the "mind control" message he found so objectionable was "Love one another, even if it's difficult."

He paused, considered this, and concluded, "Well, isn't that a message for all of us?" It was a message from headquarters.

***

Long before Dave Brubeck heard his music for the pope in a dream, he heard the message that calls us to love one another. He was raised in a very eclectic spiritual background, but love was at the core of everything he learned. Serving as a soldier to fight against Hitler's Third Reich, he was deeply troubled to see how an obsession for world domination twisted and destroyed the message of love. As he reflected later in life,

> The idiocy of the entire Christian world bent on fratricide, rather than brotherhood, leads me to believe that we have missed the whole point of Jesus' life. I puzzled as a young soldier twenty-five years ago (as I do now) at Christians who can still think in terms of "the enemy," forgetting that devout prayers are being offered to the One God from both sides of the battle. In God's eyes can there be an enemy?

> A peaceful and merciful world seems to me as credible as Hitler's army of hate. We can sure enlighten and prepare for a cause more natural to man's spirit.

This vision of holy love nurtured much of Brubeck's own creativity. He perceived divine creativity as an expression of God's love, love as the origin of life, the purpose of life, the greatest truth of life, and the ultimate destiny of life.

To perceive God as Creator is to affirm the generous benevolence of One too great for us to see but not so distant for us to ignore. Our origin is an expression of the love of the Creator. None of us *needed* to exist. The fact that we do is a sign of the effusive love of the unseen God, who calls us to echo that love in all that we create. And that is difficult.

Years ago, I had the opportunity to look over the original manuscripts in Dave Brubeck's archives. Many were musical settings of biblical texts. One was his handwritten setting of Jesus's exhortation "Love your enemies, do good to those who hate you." He gave it a strange melody with odd intervals, sounding the harsh demand of the text. Musically, you could "hear" Brubeck saying the command is arduous but possible. And it requires a lot of practice to get it right.

***

When we hear music, particularly music that creates as it proceeds, we are given an opportunity to hear the message from headquarters for ourselves. This can renew and realign our own spiritual imagination.

British music critic Michael Tucker writes about the power of jazz to awaken values in a world that has largely burned out on religion and no longer regards churches as sacred sanctuaries of the creative holy. He turns his attention to the ECM record label and its music, much of it jazz with a European bent and most of it expansive, even mystical. A prolific label, ECM maintains extremely high production values and offers a roster of luminous musicians from around the globe. Tucker compares the music he hears on those recordings to the films of Ingmar Bergman, the brilliant filmmaker who created haunting images of a postmodern world that has experienced the "withdrawal of the Protestant God":

> Though certain, as (Bergman) said, that "God is dead," he spoke of his conviction that in every human being there is "a room that is holy," a room "very high," "very secret." Here—in the sense of an inner transreligious spiritual potential that may be nourished, in good part by the world of art—is perhaps the point where Bergman's work most profoundly touches that of Eicher and ECM.

Tucker hears a sounding that beckons all of us toward what he calls "True North." He understands this as a grounding in values, a pointing toward what is real despite the shadows of this world. The arts utilize imagination to speak truth, uncover illusion, voice pain, point to beauty, and sing of relief and repair. We hear the saxophonist wail about injustice. Or the bassist bowing out beauty. There is a deep resonance between the Source of living music and the pursuits of the human heart. There is something—dare we say *Spirit*?—alive at the center of it all.

Many in the jazz world cannot say the word *God*. They see that religion has often been employed as a straitjacket of freedom, a tool of bigotry, and a weapon of destruction. I have a great sensitivity for those people hurt by churches and those who presume to lead them. That sensitivity and belief in an ongoing creation lead me to echo, as theologian Paul Tillich suggested many years ago, that there is a "God above God." Behind the transcendent experience, beneath it, and certainly ahead of it, there is Something true, pure, loving, and holy.

Call me a closet Platonist, but I believe there is a realm of beauty and joy that is just out of our reach. An artist aspires to touch these things without clinging to them. That's why those of us who are musicians create with the tips of our fingers or on the edge of our lips. We can touch the music beyond us, but we also understand we can never possess or control it.

And for all who listen, there is the real possibility that the music bears the power to enlighten, energize, and even lift our souls. As one author notes, "Jazz answered needs that traditional faiths did not address. While the music had different meanings for different followers—black or white, male or female, young or old, rich or poor, in various psychological states and social situations—for all devotees it provided some form of ecstasy or catharsis transcending the limitations, dreariness, and desperation of ordinary existence."

This is the message from headquarters for us. It bears the promise that the universe is not closed, the fix is not in, and hope is not a sham. Life continues to surge from the Source. Even when a situation seems lost, it is still infused with possibility.

Pianist Herbie Hancock recounts the night he performed with the Miles Davis Quintet in Stockholm. They were playing Miles's famous tune "So What," and the band was cooking that night. Ron Carter's nimble bass lines drove the beat. Tony Williams thundered on his drums. With Herbie, they created a magic carpet that soared higher and higher as Miles crackled a burning solo.

Then it happened. Herbie hit a chord that was, in his words, "one hundred percent wrong." Miles paused as the pianist cursed to himself, fearful he had destroyed the moment. Then Miles played some notes that made Herbie's chord sound right. Miles launched his solo in a new trajectory, drawing inspiration from the wrong chord and spinning fresh melodies. How did he do that?

When Hancock retold this story in his Noble Lectures at Harvard University, he said, "Miles turned my poison into medicine." Something imaginative interrupted the broken chord and spun it into a new trajectory. Magic happened. Where did it come from? To this day, Herbie has no idea. The experience rewired his circuits to believe that human life has creative, expansive possibilities. The universe is still open. And generous.

Life is infused with the possibility of liberation, justice, freedom, healing, redemption—all an ongoing creative work. This creative, free infusion is driven by Love. Jazz points us to the jazz factor, offering the necessary hints of what the Source of the universe wishes to birth among us.

Are we ready for that?

IMPROVISATION: LISTENING FOR SELAH

In the beginning was the Song,
and everybody danced.
Then Song gave birth to Words.
Faith spoke what it sang.
In the rhythm of time,
a silent battle muted all music,
and Word won for a while.
Each text lost its tune,
and faith lost its heart.
Yet Spirit speaks in Song,
and from the seeds of Word,
the Song is heard again.
For those with ears to hear,
the heart will be revived.
For those with toes to tap,
the dance goes off the page.

CHAPTER FIVE

THE SPARKS AND FLAMES OF HUMAN CREATIVITY

I don't believe that I can create, but that I can be a channel for the Creative. I *do* believe in the Creator, and so in reality this is His album through me to you, with as little in between as possible on this media-conscious earth.

—Keith Jarrett, liner notes for
Solo—Concerts: Bremen Lausanne

Your intuition and your intellect should be working together . . . making love. That's how it works best.

—Madeleine L'Engle

CRISIS IN COLOGNE, REDEEMED

Vera Brandes was distraught. The prestigious opera house in Cologne, Germany, had been less than enthusiastic about renting out its hall for a jazz concert. Vera had to schedule the show for 11:00 p.m. The piano she rented had not been delivered. In a comedy of errors, a tiny facsimile of the preferred Bosendorfer Imperial Concert Grand sat on stage, out of tune and virtually unplayable. Keys were sticking. The pedals didn't work.

What if she had to cancel the concert at the last minute?

If all that wasn't enough, the concert artist was furious and ready to call off the concert.

Vera stepped to the curb again to talk to pianist Keith Jarrett, who sat in a small Peugeot with his producer. They were tired from a long drive to northern Germany from Switzerland. They were hungry after a terrible meal in an Italian restaurant.

Standing in the rain, Vera pleaded with Jarrett. "Please play for us! We have sold out all fourteen hundred seats and have no way to refund the tickets. I have done everything I can to make this concert happen. And a piano tuner is on his way."

Jarrett looked at her, turned to his producer, and pivoted back to Vera, who was drenched from the rain.

He raised one finger, looked her in the eye, and replied, "Never forget. Only for you."

For several hours, a piano tuner worked tirelessly, doing what he could with an instrument long neglected and damaged, a castoff piano that someone on the opera house staff had evidently assumed would be adequate for a jazz concert. Later that night, Jarrett played a sixty-six-minute concert on that piano that was completely improvised. He had no musical score, no tune list. Yet the music poured out of him.

"The Koln Concert" became a hit well beyond the fourteen hundred seats. The show was recorded and released and would go on to become the best-selling jazz piano recording of all time.

Obviously, the piano tuner worked some magic.

So did Keith Jarrett. His inventions enchanted the crowd in that hall and cast a spell on the millions of listeners who would later buy the recording. Pure imagination.

In jazz, we meet the mystery of human creativity, bequeathed to us by the Divine. In visual form, this mystery and creativity are well represented by that life-giving spark between God and Adam painted on the ceiling of the Sistine Chapel. That seemingly empty space is one I consider to be the creative spark, a gift from the Holy, by which the human family participates on the eighth day of creation. We dream of possibilities. We imagine alternatives. We make things. We give birth. Our human imagination is sparked by the Creative Source.

HAVE A LITTLE TALK

One observer of the Koln concert identifies the opening five notes of Jarrett's improvisation—a familiar sound quoting the tones played in the lobby of the opera house inviting audience members to take their seats. Consciously or unconsciously, Keith picked that short phrase, created a few variations, and launched into a twenty-six-minute exploration.

At the end of the concert, Jarrett played an untitled encore. He stated the melody a few times and stuck to the twenty-four-measure sequence of chords as he improvised. While nobody recalls if he had ever played this tune before or after that concert, it is clear he had worked it out before this performance. The album titles the encore "IIc." Jarrett had a musical conversation with his own tune.

Part of the magic of creativity happens in dialogue. The improviser begins a conversation with the scrap of a tune, or a sequence of harmonies, or an experience within the room, or tones calling an audience to take a seat. That's when something new happens.

Among jazz legends, there is a story about the trumpeter Wynton Marsalis. It comes from a season in his career when he had dropped out of sight for a while. Journalist David Hajdu went out one night in August to listen to a band assembled by a little-known saxophonist. Standing in the shadows of the nightclub stage was the band's trumpeter. It looked like Wynton. He wore an expensive Italian suit, as Marsalis would have, but he was pudgier than Hajdu remembered. The musician was middle-aged and without as much hair as Hajdu remembered. And if this was Marsalis, his eyes had since lost their old glimmer.

The next tune was his featured solo. He stepped up to play the ballad "I Don't Stand a Ghost of a Chance with You." It was a sad song, which Wynton played without accompaniment. The performance was breathtaking. The inflections had traces of melancholy as he spoke through his horn. As Marsalis reached the climax, he played the final phrase in a deliberate tone: "I don't stand . . . a ghost . . . of . . . a . . . chance." The room was completely still.

Just then, somebody's cell phone went off with a dorky ringtone, a melody with electronic bleeps. The audience giggled. People reached for their drinks. The spell was broken but not for Marsalis. He paused, motionless, his eyebrows arched, as the journalist scribbled a note, "Magic, ruined." Then Marsalis, still at the microphone, replayed the stupid cell phone melody note for note, repeated it, and started to improvise variations on it. The audience put down their drinks and leaned forward.

He changed the key, played another variation, turned the variation upside down, changed the key again. With a flurry of notes, he settled back down to a slow tempo, ending up exactly where he had let off: "with . . . you." The room exploded with applause. People stood up and cheered.

The assumption that the old song had been ruined was flipped on its head—because Wynton's creative juices had taken that old song somewhere new.

BLESSING THE MESS

Reflecting on Keith Jarrett's 1975 concert at the Cologne Opera House, writer Tim Harford offers insight into the truth of creativity:

> Keith Jarrett had been handed a mess. He'd embraced that mess, and it soared. But let's think for a moment about Jarrett's initial instinct. He didn't want to play. Of course. I think any of us in any remotely similar situation would feel the same way. We'd have the same instinct. But Jarrett's instinct was wrong. And I think our instinct is also wrong. I think we need to gain a bit more appreciation for the unexpected advantages of having to cope with a little mess.

In the messes that find us, there is a pregnant moment of ambiguity when we ask ourselves, What are we going to do? What comes next?

Rather than freeze, we can appreciate those unexpected moments of mess. We can choose to jump in, engage, dance with the moment, and discover what comes next. The creative occasion, whether Divine or human, often proceeds as a narrative, punctuated with the phrase "and then . . . and then."

We can experience this through simple games, a variation on the "yes, and . . ." method of improvisation. It is a variation for stage, music, and long car rides. I often try to lean into improvisation, well, anywhere. When my children were young, complaining of boredom on a long car ride, I would jump in, saying, "Let's make up a story."

Then I established a scene: "A young woman went out in a canoe. As she paddled down the river, she noticed the current was moving faster and faster. And then . . ."

One of the kids would add, "She could see the rapids ahead, so she leaned forward and braced herself. Suddenly she realized there was a small leak in the canoe. And then . . ."

Her sister, taking the cue, said, "She pulled the Double Bubble chewing gum out of her mouth and plugged the hole. Whew! That was when she spotted the waterfall up ahead. And then . . ."

Creativity evolves in dialogue. And if we dwell long enough in the narrative dream of story, of music, new twists and turns emerge. The plot develops in expected and delightful ways.

Years after the car-ride story, I discovered the creativity research of Mihaly Csikszentmihalyi, a professor at the University of Chicago, who brought a now recognizable term to the understanding of creativity: "What makes experiences in life genuinely satisfying is a state of consciousness called 'flow.' A state of concentration so focused (without overthinking or analyzing) that it amounts to absolute absorption in an activity. Total immersion in whatever you are doing."

This explains why the saxophonist improvises a long solo and the car ride suddenly sped by for my family. Creativity invites us into an experience of total immersion. When we are in a state of flow, we can lose all track of time. Or, better stated, we can step out of clock time into an experience of eternity.

***

Spontaneous composition—that's how I describe improvisation to my music students. The imagination is uncorked. Many beginners freeze when it's their turn to jump into the "flow" being created in a dialogue. Occasionally, students will bolt from the room, fearfully exclaiming, "I can't do that!"

To create, we are called on to step beyond fear, whether it comes from perfectionist tendencies or anxieties about failure—which are probably the same thing. Some creatives even view fear as an impetus for the work, seeing barriers as challenges. When we blast through the yellow caution tape, when we dismiss the little voice that says, "I am not creative," we grow, we create, we connect to that Sacred Spark of the divine Creator.

"When I drop my hands on the piano," says pianist Kenny Werner, "no matter what comes out, I say, 'That is the most beautiful sound I've ever heard . . .' Sound is neither good or bad, beautiful or ugly. We superimpose those values onto it. You will find yourself far more free and powerful if you assume that all notes you play are the most beautiful sounds you've ever heard."

This philosophy readies the spirit to be open to whatever comes. To receive what comes as a gift. To welcome the sounds we make as a matter of significance. To accept them without critique or analysis. Creative flow can be short-circuited by internal criticism, but it is frequently released when the creator feels freedom.

DOES YOUR BRAIN WORK DIFFERENTLY THAN MINE?

Dr. Charles Limb is an ear, nose, and throat doctor and brain scientist. He is also a jazz fan. Intrigued by the creative process, he put jazz pianists in an MRI machine and mapped what happened in their brains when they made music.

First, he asked them to play a piece they had memorized. After that, he handed them a specially designed keyboard and asked them to improvise with another musician in the control room. When the musicians began to improvise, two things happened. "Musicians were turning off the self-censoring part of the brain so they could generate novel ideas without restrictions," he notes. At the same time, the part of the brain that processes language lit up like a Christmas tree. If you recall Paul Berliner's earlier observation that jazz functions linguistically, you'll recognize that connection here. It is a musical form of speech. It is a vehicle of communication akin to dialogue.

Human creativity, Dr. Limb believes, can be developed, especially with children—and those who wish to be more like children. Choosing to be playful is one key. Carving out unstructured time is another. And best of all for creativity? Engaging in spontaneous conversations, musical or otherwise.

At a conference of neuroscientists in San Diego, Limb welcomed guitarist Pat Metheny to the podium. Metheny described himself in his keynote address as a professional improviser, noting he worked in the magical, elusive space "where the brain meets the soul." In the ensuing conversation, Pat discussed how it is difficult to talk about melody, even if most people recognize it. He likened it to telling a story:

> To me, that's the glue that connects to ideas. And the way you express time in a narrative way is the thing that I think makes it accessible. . . . That quality is absolutely central to Miles Davis, Ornette Coleman, and on and on. There is a clarity of intent and purpose in their narrative expositions that is very, very close to what storytelling is.

THE MUSIC PLAYS THE MUSICIAN

Metheny's words remind me of a night when some friends joined me to hear him tell some musical stories. We sat in a crowded university gymnasium as Pat took the stage. Surrounded by a band of stellar musicians, he launched into a long guitar solo and took us with him. It sped along furiously like a roller-coaster ride. We hung on over every angular bump and surprising turn. And he kept going.

The woman next to me was dazzled. She leaned over to exclaim, "How is this happening?" Not the most precise question, but I understood what she asked. Metheny played as if he was possessed. As if an angel had taken control of his abilities.

We were in the presence of something mystical, something powerful yet personal.

In such moments, I remember the occasional religious texts in which musicians and other artists are visited by a Creative Presence. In the Hebrew book of Proverbs, this Presence is named Lady Wisdom and identified as the first of God's creation:

> The Lord created me at the beginning of his work, the first
>   of his acts of long ago.
> Ages ago I was set up, at the first, before the beginning of
>   the earth.
> When there were no depths I was brought forth,
> when there were no springs abounding with water.
> Before the mountains had been shaped, before the hills, I
>   was brought forth.

More than a message from headquarters, Wisdom is a presence, a gift, a means of empowerment by which mere mortals participate in the overflowing joy of the divine. "When God marked the foundations of the earth," she says, "I was daily his delight, rejoicing before him always, rejoicing in his inhabited world and delighting in the human race."

When the sparks of ingenuity fly, the sage of Proverbs suggests it may be an experience of visitation, a moment of inspiration that comes bidden or unbidden, when insight explodes, and the human creator becomes a conduit for something that originates from beyond us. We don't often have the language to describe what happens, but this is a genuine experience of imaginative souls.

As this chapter's epigraph by Keith Jarrett echoes, "I don't believe that I can create, but that I can be a channel for the Creative."

The work of imaginative souls is in directing attention to a deeper Source. The improviser's gift, cultivated through developing musical tools, is availability.

Gary Peacock played bass in Jarrett's trio for nearly thirty-five years. As a practitioner of Zen Buddhism, he described the creative moment this way: "First, the music enters us. And if the music enters you, then you don't have to worry so much about what to play. The music is telling you what to play."

For anyone who approaches music-making with scientific precision, this language may sound confusing. Years of practice can develop fluidity on any musical instrument. Yet, without the spark, the dialogue, the channel, the temptation creeps in to regard oneself as a master, to play notes that have been played before, to rely on clichés that the listeners have not heard before, and to create the illusion that we are creative when we are not.

Jarrett, Peacock, and countless others point to a deeper process, that of emptying our preconceived ideas to receive what might come as a gift. Musicians who remain open and available can often perceive themselves as conduits for music that originates from a deeper Source. When swept up into the flow, they can welcome what the Creator wishes to sing *through* them. The music cannot be forced.

As someone once observed about the creativity of trombonist Bob Brookmeyer, "Music will happen according to a logic of its own, as long as you are ready—and have developed the tools—to receive it."

THE NECESSITY OF DISCERNMENT

Discovering creativity can be exhilarating, exciting—and enticing. But for us to come completely alive, there must be discernment, a truthful view of what will give life and what will not. Imagination is a holy gift, and it can be misused. There are grim reminders of this throughout history and scripture.

In the book of Proverbs, Lady Wisdom reminds us to return to the divine Source:

> For whoever finds me finds life and obtains favor from the
>   Lord;
> But those who miss me injure themselves.

Every imaginative artist can make something beautiful but also faces the temptation to make something ugly. Even though human creativity comes from the Source, it can be twisted out of shape and used to participate in evil. This is a matter of truthfulness, of creating music that resonates with its Source.

David Friesen is a world-class jazz bassist based in the Pacific Northwest. In his music workshops, he challenges jazz musicians to claim the life-giving qualities of what they create. Friesen believes music is a holy gift that strengthens and enriches human life. It promises to reveal what is real and heal what is fractured. "But if the musician isn't honest about these purposes," he notes, "or if there is any confusion, it affects the feeling of the music, that [indescribable quality] in the note that heals, comforts and builds up."

Friesen echoes the observations of the late Eugene Peterson, spiritual writer and sage, who wrote, "The imagination is among the chief glories of the human. When it is healthy and energetic, it ushers us into adoration and wonder, into the mysteries of God. When it is neurotic and sluggish, it turns people, millions of them, into parasites, copycats, and couch potatoes."

In the days after the 9/11 attacks, I had dinner with an architect who brought disturbing insight into how imagination can be distorted toward destruction. The terrorists knew exactly what they were doing, the architect said.

"Most people would think you take down a building the same way you chop down a tree: by striking at the bottom," he told me. "These guys learned enough architecture to know the more effective way to destroy a skyscraper is to hit it at the top and watch it collapse under its own weight."

The observation was stunning. Human imagination can be enlisted for profound evil. Suddenly I realized why all the destructive plots in spy thrillers and James Bond films were so captivating to me. The highest thoughts and most creative connections can be twisted into acts of damage and devastation. They are ingenious. And deadly.

Yet I also understand why music is so powerful for so many of us. Melody can lift us into a greater Light. Harmony offers depth and substance. Rhythm forms a sense of community out of isolation. The music beckons us into an unfolding story that will change us for the better.

And discernment seeks the truth about what will invite us to thrive.

John Coltrane certainly understood the power of his creative work. Interviewed eight months before his death, he was asked about his sense of purpose for his music as well as his life. And his reply is the last word on the matter: "I want to be a force for real good. In other words, I know that there are bad forces. I know that there are forces out here that bring suffering to others and misery to the world, but I want to be the opposite force. I want to be the force which is truly for good."

At this, Lady Wisdom smiles. She rejoices whenever the Creator's generous imagination has sparked the imagination of the creators.

IMPROVISATION: REFRACTED LIGHT

There are eighty-three ways
to see
the furrowed brow
the risky decision
the red pomegranate.

Let me harmonize the single note
in seventy-nine ways,
adding incognito cluster
or obscure sound.
This gives it gristle.

If Adam named eight million animals
in order to control them,
he should have kept
his mouth shut,
especially around the tigers.

Can we spin a story in
sixty-seven directions?
Only if it is true.

Insight flits through
the open window.
It lights upon
a stale slice of bread,
and unveils
the banquet.

Here is the Jazz Assumption:
There must be more.

CHAPTER SIX

BROKEN BUT BEAUTIFUL

What It Means to Be Human

Jazz is music born in the pain and travail of miscarried lives, stillborn in the stifling darkness of dreams that cannot come to pass. Lives for whom the future is a fugitive shadow, but who still retain, in the wail of a minor key, a crescendo of hope. Thus was born soul; the mating of suffering and joy.

—John Kerr, liner notes for the recording of Eddie Bonnemere's Missa Laetere

Bix's tone was so pure, so devoid of any sentimentality or personal ego, that it was the nearest thing to perfect beauty I have ever heard.

—trumpeter Max Kaminsky on Bix Beiderbecke

Doris Day made a hit out of the tune "When I Fall in Love," and Nat King Cole charmed the world with the lyrics. But it was the Bill Evans Trio version that pierced my heart.

I first heard the album when I was in college. Having just broken up with a young woman whom I had hoped to marry, the beauty of the performance smashed through my defenses. My college music professor had told me, "You need to check out Bill Evans." And when I found his *Portrait in Jazz* recording at a music store,

I bought it and hustled back to my dorm room to listen and listen and listen again.

Evans was largely unknown to me, apart from his work on the renowned *Kind of Blue* album by Miles Davis. On this new purchase, I discovered Evans's classic trio with bassist Scott LaFaro and drummer Paul Motian. Unlike most piano trios, where bass and drums merely accompany the piano's inventions, this group created three-way musical conversations, with each musician in equal voice. Improvisations were woven from three strands.

Most of the songs were standard tunes reinvented fresh. As I listened in my dorm, notes poured into my cinder-block room. I could not take them all in. Their version of "When I Fall in Love," the final cut on the side of the album, slowed down the tempo with the ballad, and I was undone. Over a succession of half notes in the bass, Evans dropped one pearl after another. The melody slow-danced across the bar lines, never in a hurry, each note landing in the right place. His chords held the right blend of beauty and tension, supporting the melody and offering a springboard for the improvisation.

The pianist sang the lyrics through his fingers: "When I fall in love, it will be forever, or I'll never fall in love." The record concluded its play. The performance clocked in just under five minutes, but I remained frozen in time, suspended in melancholy joy. I have rarely heard anything quite so beautiful.

When Bill Evans recorded the tune, he was two years into a heroin addiction.

***

Here is one of the great mysteries of jazz. Musicians have frequently created profound beauty while their lives were in chaos, plagued by illness, addiction, poverty, despair, or complete wreckage. This has been a recurring story in the history of the genre's greatest creators. It is also the recurring story of what it means to be human—how creative work can be born of struggle.

Chet Baker, who played the trumpet with poignant beauty, was another musician imprisoned—both figuratively and literally—by heroin. With his James Dean good looks, young Baker could have been a film star. Critics and fans believed he would become the next great trumpet soloist after Miles Davis. He played with a muted flame, with a fierce tenderness that endeared him to a generation. And just as music fans were falling in love with him, he was destroying one personal relationship after another. Years of substance abuse damaged his health, rendering his appearance almost unrecognizable. Yet even after drug dealers attacked him, damaging his teeth so he couldn't play his horn, Chet Baker could still sing a ballad and melt your heart. If you asked him for an autograph, he might hit you up for money to support his heroin habit. In the end, Baker fell—or was thrown, no one knows for certain—from a hotel room balcony in Amsterdam and was left to die on the sidewalk below. The ambiguity of the tragedy suggests a backstory yet untold. "It was inevitable we would lose him that way," one musician said sadly, "because he was a complete mess." Perhaps so.

For those who live conventional and tidy lives (whatever those are), these harrowing tales have been enough for generations to instruct their children never to fall under the spell of syncopation. Certainly, that was the subtext when I announced to my parents that I wanted to play jazz. The dining room table got quiet. My dad took a deep breath and said, "Are you sure?"

I doubt that he or Mom knew of Lee Morgan, the dazzling trumpeter from Philadelphia whose prolific output is well documented on Blue Note Records. Even while spiraling into a heroin addiction he would never beat, falling in and out of poverty, Lee was a wonderful musician. He could create improvisations on the bandstand or in the studio that are studied by jazz students to this day. His life was frequently in ruins.

One night, preparing to play a gig in his hometown, Morgan shot up heroin and passed out. He fell unconscious near a hot radiator, burning his scalp. He might have died if saxophonist Wayne Shorter had not checked on him and pulled him away from the radiator. A few days later, in New Jersey, Lee performed on Shorter's first recording for Blue Note records and played some of the best solos of his life. Photos from that recording session reveal a large bandage on Morgan's scalp, covering a section of his head where he would never again be able to grow hair.

Morgan's musical reputation soared while his troubles continued until, finally, his music was silenced one winter night in Slugs, a Lower Manhattan nightclub, when his common-law wife, Helen, ended an argument with a .32 revolver. She shot him in the chest as he stepped off the stage where he was performing. He was dead at thirty-three.

From a respectable distance, it might be easy to judge and dismiss these musicians and their frequently horrifying stories. For many years, the *New Yorker* printed a disclaimer to its listings of notable concert and club bookings that happen each week in the city: "You may wish to confirm this information with the venue since musicians lead complicated lives."

Complicated, indeed. But that's not the half of it.

THE TRUTH ABOUT US

The truth was revealed to me at a breakfast buffet in a New Haven hotel. We met the morning after I gave a sermon for a symposium at the Yale Institute of Sacred Music. Palle Kongsgaard, a pastor from Denmark and fellow presenter, joined me with his breakfast tray. He thanked me for the jazz worship service that I had presented with some friends. Then he paused and said, "But I couldn't preach a sermon like yours in Copenhagen."

Palle was a notable Lutheran pastor, serving at the iconic Grundt-vig's Church in Copenhagen. He presided over jazz vespers services that pulled in young adults from the city.

He continued, "When you spoke, you said, 'The Bible tells us.' In Copenhagen, many of the people are sufficiently secular that they would say, 'What's the Bible? Why quote that? It's an old book with nothing to say to me.'"

I listened. Leaned forward. Stirred my scrambled eggs.

He went on. "You referred to God. My people would respond, 'What kind of god are you talking about? God is an archaic idea, like an old myth.'"

"Palle, what on earth do you say to your people?" I asked.

With a level gaze, he replied, "I speak about brokenness. That is the common ground where we meet. All of us are broken people." He sipped his coffee and added, "We invite the jazz to speak to our brokenness."

It was a remarkable moment of truth-telling. His wisdom resonated with the deep magic of jazz that can offer healing in the thick of tough human circumstances. He also reminded me of the writings of Henri Nouwen, the famed Dutch priest who spoke honestly of the spiritual life.

Father Nouwen believed *brokenness* was a more honest word than *sinful*. To regard something or someone else as "sinful" is to set ourselves on a false pinnacle of spiritual superiority. By contrast, Nouwen suggested that brokenness is a metaphor for our shared human condition. It can never quite be transcended—but it can lead us on a journey "toward the full realization of our humanity."

All of us are children of God, beloved and blessed by our Creator, even if our lives are in tatters. As we forge a spiritual journey, Nouwen writes,

> The great spiritual call of the Beloved Children of God is to pull their brokenness away from the shadow of the curse and put it under the light of the blessing. This is not as easy as it sounds. The powers of the darkness are strong, and our world finds it easier to manipulate self-rejecting people than self-accepting people. But when we keep listening attentively to the voice calling us the Beloved, it becomes possible to live our brokenness, not as a confirmation of our fear that we are worthless, but as an opportunity to purify and deepen the blessing that rests upon us.

Broken but beautiful. This resonates as the description of what it means to be human. To be enormously capable and deeply flawed. To be wounded and blessed. Some of us understand this as a description of ourselves. This paradox describes all of us.

THE LIVING PARADOX

Skilled jazz musicians seem to soar into the air as they play. A lifetime of practice and experience launches them into each performing moment. They spend years honing their craft, learning the musical language, and mastering their instruments. Their arduous work reveals what mere mortals can do, especially if they persevere to the point of virtuosity and creative breakthrough.

This is the blessing of being human. In the spiritual tradition, it's what we find in Psalm 8, in the most affirming words of the Bible. Speaking of the human family, the poet sings:

> You have made them a little lower than God,
> and crowned them with glory and honor.
> You have given them dominion over the works of your hands;
> you have put all things under their feet.

Looking toward heaven, the poet wonders, "Who are we, Lord, that you pay us any attention?" The answer: we are children of the Most High, created in the divine image, endowed with holy creativity. We have power and agency. We are given dominion over God's creatures. We bear the divine seal. There isn't a more noble description of humanity in all of scripture.

Yet, near to the book of Psalms is the book of Ecclesiastes, where a wise sage reflects on all that he has spent his life scrambling to attain, a process he describes as "like reaching for smoke." The sage reflects on a life of vain, empty pursuit. To paraphrase the second chapter of the book,

> I made a lot of money, and it never made me happy.
> I enjoyed the delights of the flesh, but I never knew love.
> So I worked harder, surpassed all others, and did not deny
> myself any pleasure.
> Then I watched as it all turned to sand. And it slipped
> through my fingers.

A lot of people say Ecclesiastes is a downer. I believe Ecclesiastes offers an honest corrective to self-indulgence. It punctures the myth that everything always works out well.

Ecclesiastes is a hand raised in objection to the children of God who think they can live without limits, only to find themselves consumed by their consumption. The preacher of Ecclesiastes speaks a word of wisdom to those tempted toward the foolishness of burning themselves out. The wisdom of Ecclesiastes, in the words of Henri Nouwen, is the invitation to live our brokenness under God's blessing.

Sadly, the sage's wisdom anticipated Charlie Parker, an extraordinary saxophonist who soared to the heights and fell to the depths. Nicknamed "Bird," Parker is remembered for his incredible facility on the alto saxophone and boundless imagination. He is also widely regarded as the jazz poster child for self-abuse. Dead by the age of thirty-four and mistakenly estimated by the coroner to be a sixty-five-year-old man, he never found an excess he didn't like. Bird was known for warning younger musicians, "Don't do what I do." But far too many of them refused to take that advice, believing if they lived a hard life like Bird, if they consumed life as voraciously as he did, they could play like him. Many ended up hooked on the vain dream that, in the words of Ecclesiastes, is like reaching for smoke.

And yet . . . despite his difficulties and weaknesses, Bird is revered by many of his peers as the greatest jazz musician of all time. With Dizzy Gillespie and Thelonious Monk, he invented a new musical vocabulary called *bebop*. His brilliance sparked jazz in a new direction.

Broken? Yes. But beautiful too.

CLIMBING THROUGH THE WRECKAGE

Most of the musicians of my acquaintance are remarkably nonjudgmental about the demons that can infest creative souls. All too familiar with weakness, illness, poverty, addiction, and the ensuing difficulties, they intuitively understand the paradox of what it means to be human. By sheer human determination—or the gift of divine grace—sometimes they can transcend their difficulties.

In the late 1960s, Charles Lloyd put together a game-changing quartet. From the tenor saxophone, he led a band that surfed the wave of cultural experimentation. They were headlining rock festivals at a time when many jazz groups couldn't find work. Their surging rhythms offered a soundtrack to the psychedelic shift in generations. Even before the Woodstock Festival, Lloyd's music favored love, not war, even if that meant rebellion against authority. His quartet hit it *big*.

Then, suddenly, he quit.

Just like that, Charles Lloyd abruptly broke up the band and vanished. At the peak of his career, he went into a self-imposed exile, moving to the Big Sur wilderness of California. Those who discussed his disappearance gave varying explanations. He was burned out. His record company treated him like a "product." He had expended energy reaching toward the heavens and found himself grounded on earth.

Later, Lloyd reflected on that time: "I began to pull back with non-prescription drugs. I started to medicate myself; it sneaks up on you. You don't know that this tragic magic is indeed tragic." In a moving moment, he admits,

> I hit a wall. I couldn't really function. And the music business was very disenchanting to me at that time. I just disbanded the group. I had wonderful musicians, but by that time, I was falling apart. At a certain point, I began to suffer musically, and I began to suffer personally, and I was off my spiritual compass, and I could feel it. And it disturbed me. I had to go away. I could tell.
>
> I was determined to get my spiritual life back and that original inspiration that fueled me. I planted gardens, pulled weeds—both literally and metaphorically—and swept the dust away.

One day, just as suddenly, he returned. His feet were on the ground. His eyes shone. His soul had expanded. There was a depth, substance, and peace in his horn. His music had a quiet authority.

Five months after the terrorist attacks of September 11, 2001, Lloyd assembled a band in the recording studio to create two hours of consolation for the world. In *Lift Every Voice and Sing*, an album named after a hymn he recorded that day, he included his take on "Amazing Grace," as well as the spirituals "Deep River" and "Go Down Moses."

As one reviewer of that recording commented, "Lloyd's largesse here is his sincerity. The distinctness of this music is a break from the artificiality of many responses to 9/11. Lloyd's belief in humanity and reliance on the healing and redemptive qualities of music propels this compassionate recording."

Broken? Yes. But beautiful. This is a resonant gift that jazz can offer.

Before Keith Jarrett began playing solo piano concerts like the one described in the last chapter, he performed with Lloyd's first globetrotting quartet. His highly productive career was interrupted by a debilitating bout with chronic fatigue syndrome that began in 1996. He described it many times "as if aliens invaded my body." He had no energy to play, no strength to pull the cover off the piano in his studio, and no desire to leave the house for the better part of two years.

After attempting to treat this bacterial parasite with a fierce regimen of aggressive medications, vitamins, and dietary supplements, the day came when he decided to fight back. Keith crawled across his property to the barn studio he had set up, turned on a digital tape recorder, and played brief, simple interpretations of songs with strong melodies. He recounts the story on film, saying, "I was telling the disease, 'I know you're here, I have accepted your presence, and I am still going ahead with this work.' I was transforming my disease into a song."

One Christmas Day, he presented his wife, Rose Ann, with a small package. It was a wrapped set of digital recording tapes. "I couldn't leave the house to get her a Christmas gift," he explained. So he gave her what he could, the result of extraordinary labor, sometimes recording only a few minutes at a time. Moved to tears, she witnessed his recovery continuing. And the gift he shared was later released as the commercial recording *The Melody at Night, with You.*

When everything superfluous is stripped away, when we face our brokenness with honesty and vulnerability, our souls can open to deeper honesty.

SOMETIMES BEAUTY IS WROUGHT FROM PAIN

When we give up the need to impress or strive, and simply confess the truth of who we are and where we are broken, it can open us to the possibility of beauty. Other times, our fragile nature is disclosed despite heroic efforts to deny our fragility.

In Peter Pettinger's biography of pianist Bill Evans, he recounts an event in 1963 when the pianist, in need of money, took a weeklong engagement at the Village Vanguard, one of the premier jazz venues in New York City. Before leaving for the engagement, Evans shot some heroin into his right arm. He hit a nerve, and his arm went dead. But a gig is still a gig, especially if you need the money, so he went to the Vanguard and played the entire week with one hand. Evans was such an extraordinary pianist that many listeners didn't even know. The word spread around town, and local pianists lined up to see this ghastly spectacle. As bassist Bill Crow recounted, "If you looked away, you couldn't tell anything was wrong."

As I first discovered by listening to his recording of "When I Fall in Love," Bill Evans created beautiful music—music you intuitively knew came from a deep place, deeper than his tortured soul. He struggled to beat his addictions, but the gravitational pull was stronger than his will. He struggled with the demands of constant touring and lifelong feelings of inferiority. His life was also torn apart by a series of tragedies at critical moments in his career, including the sudden death of his favorite bassist, Scott LaFaro, in a car crash and the suicides of his common-law wife, Ellaine, and his brother Harry Evans. For a sensitive soul like Evans, the losses were debilitating.

Evans's addictions would lead to an early death. But there was something else. His one-time girlfriend Peri Cousins reported that Evans knew his addiction was self-destructive. It rearranged his energy and time and became a financial drain. He felt imprisoned by the heroin and helpless to stop. Cousins observed, "When he came down, when he kicked it, which he did on numerous occasions, the world was—I don't know how to say it—too beautiful. It was too sharp for him. It's almost as if he had to blur the world for himself by being strung out. I had that impression all the time."

Other musicians worked hard to chase away their demons, with mixed results. We discussed John Coltrane's story in an earlier chapter. Miles Davis fought his own heroin addiction on his father's farm in East Saint Louis but never outlived his taste for cognac. Or painkillers. Or cocaine. Bud Powell and Thelonious Monk, two brilliant pianists, wrestled with serious mental illnesses that rendered each of them nearly catatonic on occasion. Yet none of these artists ever stopped creating.

But then there's the story of Bix Beiderbecke.

TARNISHED BEAUTY

It was the sound of Bix's cornet that caught everybody's attention. One composer described it as a "padded mallet striking a chime." Someone else said it sounded "like pearls falling into velvet."

Musician Eddie Condon said, "Beiderbecke took out a silver cornet. He put it to his lips and blew a phrase. The sound came out like a girl saying yes."

Born when jazz was still in its infancy, Leon "Bix" Beiderbecke was baptized in the First Presbyterian Church of Davenport, Iowa, where his mother played the organ on Sunday mornings and his father had an account for delivering coal. As a young toddler, Bix could pick notes out of the air and play them on the family piano. In fact, he was so naturally musical that he never really developed the ability to read the dots on the page. He simply had the gift to put the notes in the air.

Bix's pain began early. When he played, the atmosphere was full of excitement. But while the world would one day praise his jazz, he never heard a complimentary word from the parents who otherwise loved him. His father thought music was a fickle mistress, a complete waste of time. Playing his cornet was the one thing Bix loved most, and it became the one thing his parents tried to get him to stop doing. Music was fine for church on Sunday morning, but the rest of the week was a time for productivity. His German father was relentless in insisting that Bix get a so-called real job, but it only hardened the boy's resolve. After a troubling event with the law, Bix was sent to a military academy near Chicago, only to be expelled after being caught on the fire escape, sneaking back in after a night of Chicago jazz.

His parents were beside themselves. They tried to interest him in the family coal business, which would have made him wealthy, but soon Bix hopped a train with his horn. And wherever he rode after that, a bottle of Prohibition-era homemade gin was often close at hand. For Beiderbecke, the evidence of his wounds poured from a bottle.

Over time, Bix made a name for himself. He claimed the jazz trumpet chair in the Paul Whiteman Orchestra, the premier New York band of the Roaring Twenties. But the greater his fame, the more his family despised it. In a time before interstate highways, he traveled widely to the acclaim of thousands but retired each night to a lonely hotel. In the pearls that poured from his horn, you can hear a trace of melancholy, a gap between the dream and the reality. He made over 150 recordings and regularly sent copies home to Davenport, even as the drinking got worse, causing a physical breakdown. Eventually, Whiteman sent him home to recuperate at his family home, where his parents reopened the door.

Then one day, still in his bathrobe, Bix opened a hall closet of his family home and discovered copies of his records, still unopened in their original packages. At the time, his cornet playing was rivaled only by Louis Armstrong, who admired him deeply. Yet his parents disapproved so thoroughly that they wouldn't even listen to the recordings making him world-famous.

Bix drank himself to an early grave. He died at the age of twenty-eight from years of self-administered alcohol poisoning.

We all have the capacity for giving and receiving deep love but only within the most fragile of relationships. We bear the power to make beautiful things, but even in the beauty, there is a trace of melancholy.

All of us know what this is like. No one is exempt from weakness. We all have our wounds. When it comes to art, when it comes to faith, maybe this is how it is.

Still, the musicians persist. Still, they create, refusing to let their limitations silence them. This is a human mystery, and I take it to be one of the deep mysteries of the spiritual life. No matter how damaged, no matter how fragile, there remains a spark of life, a flickering testament to divine power.

TREASURE IN FRAGILE CLAY JARS

In a painful section of one of his letters, the apostle Paul remembers how many times he has been beaten up by the world. Yet the spark is still alive within him.

For Paul, there was a greater power at work. He knew a strength that was greater than his own. He affirmed there was no way he could keep doing what he was doing unless God was at work in him. "We have this treasure in clay jars," the apostle wrote, "so that it may be made clear that this extraordinary power belongs to God and does not come from us."

This is the paradox—the tarnished beauty, the fragile strength. The power of the Creator found in a beaten-up apostle, found in an infant in swaddling clothes, the complete justice of God condemned by cynical politicians, the very gift of life condemned by the powers of death. Great treasure often comes in a fragile package.

Throughout the living history of jazz, there is a long tradition of musicians being undervalued despite spinning marvelous notes. They are afflicted in every way—personal troubles, poverty-level wages, and those who take advantage of their gifts for commercial gain—yet they persist in making music. They are perplexed by insensitivity, thoughtlessness, and superficiality, but they do not despair the art. They are persecuted by those who critique music they do not understand, yet the music will not leave these musicians alone. They may be struck down by illness, indifference, even addiction, but their music will not be destroyed.

There is a deep joy within the most imperfect of praise-makers.

Bix Beiderbecke spent his final days in a rooming house in Queens. The bathtub gin had become more important than his friends. He was a long way from Davenport, lost to the family he loved. Yet even then, his landlord reports, Bix picked up his cornet at all hours of day and night, and he would play. The tenants in the building would mention to the landlord that they had been awakened at two or three in the morning by lovely music coming out of that apartment. Then they quickly added, "Please don't mention we said anything; we don't want him to get in trouble, and we also don't want him to stop."

How broken, how beautiful, how free.

IMPROVISATION: LESSON IN DISSONANCE

She pushes
down two
adjacent piano keys,
flinches,
declaring,
"That's ugly."

Maybe.

Any two notes
side by side
could bite one another
in bitter harmony.

Play them again.
Sustain the cluster.
Let tension ring.
Still ugly, perhaps.
Resolution will
not come easily.

Like hearts
out of phase.

Hit them again,
Together,
pedal to the floor,
tension sustained.
Perceiving the unheard
reference tone.
Now vibrations
resonate.
Strings hum
with one another.
Beauty is hidden
in the dissonance.

Listen until
you hear it.
Listen again.

CHAPTER SEVEN

THAT HEALIN' FEELIN'
The Soundtrack of Restoration

God helps people through jazz; people have been healed through it.
It has happened to me.

—*Mary Lou Williams*

A musical performance softens hard hearts, leads in the humor of
reconciliation, and summons the Holy Spirit.

—*Hildegard of Bingen*

FACING THE UNSPEAKABLE

Jimmy Greene remembers the phone call no parent should ever
have to receive. His wife, Nelba, said, "There's been a shooting at
our elementary school. Can you go to the volunteer fire department
next to the school and see what's going on?"

Greene, a renowned saxophonist, immediately left his office at
Western Connecticut State University. Fearful for his daughter, Ana
Grace, and his son, Isaiah, he rushed to the command center adjacent
to the Sandy Hook Elementary School. He was waved through the
barricades and flashing lights and entered a chaotic scene. Some of
the parents were reunited with their children, while others begged

for answers. Jimmy found Isaiah, gave him a huge hug, and asked, "Where's your sister?" There was no news.

Hours later, the worst was confirmed. A deranged shooter had murdered Ana Grace along with nineteen of her classmates and six adults after shooting his own mother and before turning the gun on himself.

The mass shooting of December 14, 2012, at Sandy Hook Elementary School rocked the nation. The tragedy was senseless. Jimmy and Nelba lost their six-year-old girl.

That day, only two things made sense to him. The first was a community of support as family members, friends, and musical colleagues surrounded him. Along with love from their church family, the jazz community stood with the family in their grief. The Marsalis brothers, Wynton and Branford, were among the first of hundreds to send messages. Harry Connick Jr., the famed pianist who employed Jimmy for his band, appeared at the door and sat beside Isaiah to have a talk. Bassist John Patitucci, a devout Christian, visited with Jimmy and prayed with him.

The second was an unexpected gift to Jimmy from his daughter. Before leaving for school, she had drawn colorful pictures of flowers and stapled together a booklet. The cover read "Ana's Flower Book—From Ana to Dad." She had worked on it for days, hiding it from her father when he entered the room and leaving it for him to find as a surprise to brighten his day.

In the weeks following the tragedy, one more gift emerged: a message to sustain Jimmy and his family. His wife, Nelba Márquez-Greene, explains, "I don't even remember how it all got started; I just remember it became a chant in our house shortly after the shooting. We needed to keep Ana alive. We needed to keep her spirit with us." They began to repeat a household refrain, "Love wins."

The chant grew into a song with the same title, a collaboration recorded by Greene and Connick Jr. In the following months, Jimmy composed a series of new tunes, which resulted in two recordings as a memorial to Ana Grace. The first, *A Beautiful Life*, was nominated for two Grammy awards with the music that offered a way for a grieving father to express his sorrow as well as celebrate his daughter's life and the joy she freely shared. As he told a reporter, "Music is extremely helpful dealing with the complex emotions that the grief process brings on."

Even with healing, tears still come. Ana Grace's absence is real. Her brother now grows up as an only child. "I still think of my little girl every moment of every day," Jimmy says. And every day, he keeps playing music to work through his loss.

ROOTS DEEP IN SUFFERING

When she taught jazz history, pianist Mary Lou Williams described the tradition as a massive tree with many branches. The artist David Stone Martin depicted her vision in a poster, with the trunk of the tree extending up through jazz history: "Spirituals—Ragtime—KC Swing—Bop." Beneath it all, reaching deeply into the soil, the tree's roots are unmistakably labeled "Suffering." On all sides of the trunk, "Blues" is inscribed.

Williams's manager, Father Peter F. O'Brien, SJ, explains:

> The importance of the blues cannot be overemphasized in Williams' music. She would often say: "What I'm trying to do is bring back good jazz to you with the healing in it and spiritual feeling," and, "The blues was really important—this is your healing and love in the music." In her teaching and talking about jazz, she never tired of pointing toward "this feeling." She'd say, "It's all spiritual music and healing to the soul." Part of this was in defiance of those who would call jazz "the devil's music," and part was in defiance of those who would play jazz filled with technique but very little feeling.

Jazz is not afraid of pain. In fact, for Mary Lou, the music that best addresses suffering is the music first rooted in suffering. Williams, a venerable figure in jazz history, described herself as the only pianist to perform through the first six decades of the music's development. She was an astounding jazz pianist. And raised in poverty, performing as a woman when most performers were male, an African American exploited by white managers, she knew pain and deprivation.

When she was traveling in Paris in 1954, she experienced a profound personal crisis. Exhausted and emotionally burned out, in the middle of a concert, she pushed back from the piano, stood up, and walked away from performing. It was the beginning of a three-year period in which she removed herself from concerts.

The event began the process of a profound religious awakening for Williams. Friends located her where she was holed up and arranged for her fare back to the United States. One of them encouraged her to start praying the Psalms. In time, her friendship with Dizzy Gillespie's wife, Lorraine, became a formative influence, and Mary Lou would convert to Roman Catholicism and spend hours in prayer.

The following year, her friend Charlie Parker was hospitalized due to his hard life of addiction. Williams was aware of Parker's long-standing troubles with heroin, but before she could intervene, he passed away.

Parker's death symbolized, as one of Williams's biographers notes, all that she had come to despise about the jazz scene in the mid-1950s: lack of personal accountability, self-absorption, and an indifference to human needs. His death, combined with her sensitivity to the needs of the jazz community, prompted her to turn her newfound faith into action. She turned her small apartment into a one-woman detox center, feeding, clothing, and finding gigs for down-and-out musicians. She refused to sit passively while her fellow musicians fell into ruin.

Dizzy Gillespie and others encouraged her to return to performing, which she did with renewed energy. She began to compose jazz with religious influences, first in 1963 as a tribute to Saint Martin de Porres—the first patron saint of multiracial peoples—and then the music for three jazz masses. Mary Lou offered her blues-infused compositions as spiritual medicine for those troubled and afflicted.

To ensure that no listener missed the point of her music, she distributed a mimeographed sheet at her performances entitled "Jazz for the Soul." At the bottom of the page, the following message was printed in block letters: "YOUR ATTENTIVE PARTICIPATION, THRU LISTENING WITH YOUR EARS AND YOUR HEART, WILL ALLOW YOU TO ENJOY FULLY THIS EXCHANGE OF IDEAS, TO SENSE THESE VARIOUS MOODS, AND TO REAP THE FULL THERAPEUTIC REWARDS THAT GOOD MUSIC ALWAYS BRINGS TO A TIRED, DISTURBED SOUL AND ALL 'WHO DIG THE SOUNDS.'"

SONGS FOR THE SOUL

Good music for a tired, disturbed soul. This was Mary Lou's gift, a musical accompaniment to her more tangible works of compassion. She was serious about supporting the healing and rehabilitation of all who struggled with unseen demons. And this facet of her work placed her within a long spiritual tradition of providing care to troubled souls through music.

One of the earliest examples of this in the biblical record is the musical therapy provided by the young shepherd David, summoned to the palace of the tormented King Saul. His playing of a stringed instrument was the only medicine to provide comfort for the king. He played music that evoked the peace of green pastures and still waters. Music stirring and confident, as befits a king who needs an emotional boost. Passionate, dazzling finger work to arouse awe.

David's musicianship is described as *skillful*, a word utilized later in the Jewish accounts as a description of an instrumentalist who has been schooled, trained, and polished. Even though tradition names David as the composer of eighty psalms, there is no mention that the shepherd boy sang any of them for the king. It was his expert, evocative string-playing that consoled Saul's soul.

Music bears this power. It invites us to immerse ourselves in sound, to welcome the cleansing, restorative rhythms of grace. We may feel tempted to consume music as a product, as a soundtrack for a romantic dinner, as the creation of a mood for a film, or as the jolly background for holiday shopping. Yet our healing will not come by consuming music as a product but by inviting the music to consume us. What true music therapy brings, as it did with David and Mary Lou Williams, is restoration of the soul.

This is the work, too, of classic jazz albums like *Kind of Blue* by the Miles Davis Sextet or *Waltz for Debby*, the live set by the Bill Evans Trio. You can picture David in the set of creative healers, plucking and strumming his strings for Saul, the Mad Despot. Substantive music is created by souls, cast into sound waves, and intended to reach other souls through the ears. It captures us in subterranean depth. It welcomes the consolation of the Holy into the crevasses of our hearts.

Among my favorite musically inclined theologians is Karl Barth, who was a serious music lover. Over time, he gravitated away from the works of Bach and leaned toward the more emotionally complex compositions of Mozart. "With Bach," he wrote, "there is always a message." Always something being preached, a doctrine or lesson within the music. By contrast, Barth noted, "Mozart does not wish to say anything; he just sings and sounds. He does not force anything on the listener, does not demand that he make any decisions or take any positions; he simply leaves him free."

That's how a soul-filled song chases away the evil spirits and puts us back together, restoring us the way we were intended to be. Freeing us from all that makes us less than human.

Just one note,
one chord,
one sound harmonizing with our souls,
and we are met
and not alone.

THE SOUNDS OF SURPRISE

Kirk Byron Jones, a Baptist preacher, admits he has had his dry spells. An outgoing, effusive man with a quick smile and twinkling eyes, he is rarely short on words. But one Saturday night, with the next morning's worship service looming larger as the hour grew later, he didn't have anything to say. No message to preach the next morning.

But this dry spell was unlike any he had ever experienced before. All other instances of writer's block faded away as, that evening, Jones grappled with the driest spell he'd ever known. For some time, he had been falling into a slump. That night, he was deep in an emotional canyon.

Jones decided to put some music on the stereo. For some reason, the usual inspirations of gospel music left him empty. As a random act, he reached for *The Intimate Ella*, a duet recording by Ella Fitzgerald and pianist Paul Smith. Then something unexpected happened; the music found his spirit, and he began to cry:

> Her angelic voice was simultaneously soft and piercing. Her singing soulfully caressed the lyrics of songs like "I Cried for You." "My Melancholy Baby" and "Reach for Tomorrow" melted my misery. This was wonderful and scary at the same time. I had been revived before, but . . . I had never been delivered by a jazz singer before. An hour later, I felt revived inside.

His story resonates with me. Years ago, in the desolation of a divorce, I had pushed myself to the point of exhaustion. I worried about my kids and how the breakup would affect them. I feared my potential financial ruin. I did not know how my beloved congregation would react to having a flawed and broken pastor.

At the bottom of that trough, I was handed a recording by Tony Marino, the bass player in my jazz quartet. All he said as he passed it along was, "Maybe you will like this."

The album was called *Officium*. It was a collaboration between the Hilliard Ensemble, a British vocal group, and Norwegian saxophonist Jan Garbarek. Recorded in a monastery chapel in the Austrian mountains, it was a rare—one might even say odd—recording. Maybe that's why Tony unloaded it on me.

The Hilliard Ensemble sang a baker's dozen of medieval ballads, one of them three separate times. Above them, Garbarek soared, weaving improvised lines around the vocal harmonies. At every turn, there were melodic surprises. The vocal settings, usually sung as dirges, were enlivened by the saxophone's inventions. Beyond that, I have no other words to describe the music. Words would only diminish it.

A seventy-seven-minute journey from start to finish, the first time I played *Officium*, it was like the time continuum collapsed. Within minutes, I shivered, wrapped myself in a blanket, and wept. The darkness enveloped me and held me close, even as a luminous Presence held me as well. When silence returned over an hour later, there was a fluttering of silent wings.

What happened? The music found me. I was discovered, known, and strangely illumined. When the lights came back on, I had been transformed somehow. If not fixed, at least mended. If not cured, at least partially soul-healed. And free.

I had discovered the intentional listening of music as a spiritual practice, as a way for the Holy to commune with us. It couldn't have happened at a better time.

THE THIN PRIEST PLAYS

Tord Gustavsen leaned into the piano, coaxing out notes with a gentle touch. His bassist anchored the harmony in slow notes while the drummer rolled mallets on the tom-toms. The group's saxophonist stood still at the center of the band, listening to the tapestry that was being woven around him.

The crowd at St. Peter's Lutheran Church was riveted. The celebrated "jazz church" lies underground at the corner of East 54th Street and Lexington Avenue in New York City. The piano was willed to the congregation by Billy Strayhorn, Duke Ellington's cocomposer. As Gustavsen caressed the ivories, years of classical technique were displayed, creating a poignant atmosphere for the hushed audience.

"I am comfortable in such a holy space," he confessed after the first song concluded. A slight, lean fellow, Gustavsen is a man of faith who speaks through his music—all kinds of music. The band's repertoire includes folk-like melodies and Scandinavian hymns, richly harmonized and deeply explored. His posture invited all of us to lean forward with him, to sink into the moment, to welcome whatever the Holiest Spirit could create.

Tord Gustavsen is a nonordained musical priest, offering his melodies as ministry. He makes himself completely available as a broker of transformation. In an interview, he said,

> I have heard so many touching reports about music making a fundamental difference in people's lives. Music can form "soundtracks" to our lives' phases. It can carry symbolic meaning and emotional triggers, filling us up, energize us, making us pensive, opening us up for reflection and meditation. And music can sometimes help people get through tragic loss. I have received several emails from people saying that one of my albums has formed a valuable companion in their journey working through grief. This really adds a fundamental aspect of the feeling that it is all "worth it" to me.

Gustavsen came to his calling through his own journey of loss. One day, his brother was driving his car down the highway with the brother's child strapped in the car seat. An erratic driver suddenly appeared in the wrong lane, speeding toward him. She hit the brother's car head on, killing him and his child.

It was the sacred gift of music that helped Gustavsen work through his grief. He played, composed, mourned—and created a suite of new compositions with titles such as "Tears Transforming," "Colors of Mercy," and "Edges of Happiness." None of the tunes in the suite moves quickly. They do not rush to superficial comfort or sweet denial of the loss. Gustavsen offers them in twinges of melancholy, painted in rich hues of patience, resilience, and quiet joy.

And they point the way through the darkness toward Light.

The Jewish mystics have given a name to that kind of light—in Hebrew, *tikkun olam* means literally "taking the world in for repairs." What scripture names in terms like *salvation* can be heard in the harp of David or in phrases that promise a future and hope. That light is what the healing power of jazz can offer in all its grit and all its joy.

The word I return to—the healing word from both scripture and jazz, pertinent to the mystery of music and its potential for healing—is *salvage*. It is the salvaging work of Mary Lou Williams, helping her peers find their way back. It is the mending of all that has been broken, the restoration of what has been twisted out of shape. It is the word that ties what is broken to salvation, offered in the promise that all things shall be made new.

IMPROVISATION:
WHAT ABOUT THE LEGS?

I say to you, stand up, take your mat, and go home.
—Mark 2:1–12

It requires special friends
to carry your limp limbs
toward Vitality.

It requires deep vulnerability
to allow yourself
to be carried.

It requires great patience
for the Teacher
to welcome
this interruption.

As the hole in the roof enlarges,
as the one who is limp is lowered,
as the day's lesson is paused,
the patient Teacher cancels . . .

. . . sins.
Sins?

As bickering experts
debate the validity of
that transaction,
another question leaps up:
What about the legs?

We do not have Redemption
if the lame cannot dance.
Start up the band.

Selah.

CHAPTER EIGHT

PRAYERS LIFTED ON A SAXOPHONE

I do feel like I'm in a prayerful mode when I'm playing, asking the Creator for food.

—*Charles Lloyd,* Horizons Touched

I am praying through my fingers when I play—and when I get the good "soul" sound, and I try to touch people's spirits.

—*Mary Lou Williams, liner notes to* Nite Life

AN UNEXPECTED BLESSING

When I was a teenager, one of our neighbors turned to look at me when his friend mentioned that I played jazz piano. "Have you heard John Coltrane's album *A Love Supreme*?" Roy asked. "That music is beautiful. It's powerful. It changed my life."

"Yeah, Coltrane is something special," I mumbled, even though, at the time, I didn't know much about the saxophonist. Nor did I have any of his recordings. Coltrane died in 1967, when I was a kid. But I made a note of the album title. After I mowed a few more lawns for pocket money, I went to the record store and found a copy of *A Love Supreme*.

It was the kind of recording that made my parents insist I wear headphones. The music was brittle, not beautiful. There was sadness and fury; there was passion and surging energy; there was pain and lack of resolution. Something was at work in that music that I—the seventeen-year-old firstborn son of an IBM executive who lived in a nice house on a hill—didn't understand. The power was undeniable, like the saxophonist took a scalpel and went right for my heart. Too much to take in.

I listened to the music a couple of times, if only to honor Roy's recommendation, but soon I set it aside.

A few months later, my father was diagnosed with a life-threatening illness. Our family's life was turned upside down. Anxiety filled our home. We didn't know if my father would survive.

For some inexplicable reason, I reached for *A Love Supreme* and listened again. This time, I heard pure honesty, raw emotion, deep devotion to God, and the possibility of grace.

Clearly, the music found me and did its work, helping heal something in my heart. And as my father met with a truly miraculous cure, I began to wonder about something more. Could jazz be a form of prayer? Not merely a soundtrack for prayer but prayer itself? Years after Coltrane's death, his ministry continued to me, in me, teaching prayer in a different form, with raw emotion, surging energy, and unresolved notes.

THE SOUNDS OF *SELAH*

In traditions such as the Eastern Orthodox branch of Christianity, scripture verses are intoned to simple chants. At an ecumenical gathering I attended, an Orthodox priest invited me to do a "reading" of scripture for evening vespers in his sanctuary. Before I began, he added, "And we *sing* the scriptures here." I found it fascinating that the only musical instrument welcomed in that sanctuary was the human voice.

From the biblical scrolls of the First and Second Chronicles, we know that instrumentalists were trained to lead the prayers of the people with cymbals, harps, and lyres. Their musical accompaniment was deemed a "ministry." Words spoken or sung required more than voices and words. In fact, on the day when the Jerusalem temple was dedicated, the Divine Presence was welcomed, not by speeches and sermons but by the sound of 120 trumpeters. According to the account,

> when the song was raised, with trumpets and cymbals and other musical instruments, in praise to the Lord, "For he is good, for his steadfast love endures forever," the house, the house of the LORD, was filled with a cloud, so that the priests could not stand to minister because of the cloud; for the glory of the LORD filled the house of God.

Instrumental music can bear this power. A well-tuned invocation is an invitation for the Holy to be revealed. Instrumentalists can amplify the Mystery that is not always obvious, one reason all the brass quartets are busy on Easter.

And yet, over the centuries, preachers and churches have skirmished with musicians, declaring the superiority of words over melodies. The battle can even be seen in the printing of the Psalms, where only words remain from the musical prayers but no tunes, save for references to melodies long forgotten. Granted, ancient Israel had no way to notate the music. But even if they had, I doubt the ancient scribes would have included them.

As a kid in Sunday School, I noticed a word in the margin of my Bible: *selah*. Our teachers told us not to read it aloud. They considered it an unnecessary word, an indecipherable smudge from an earlier edition. So whenever we saw *selah* printed in the psalms, we skipped it.

While the Hebrew word *selah* has never been adequately translated, scholars now concede that it offered ancient direction for the instrumentalists. *Selah* is a clue that something more than the spoken word was happening as psalms were prayed. *Selah* was the music that existed off the page, which was as important to the Jewish prayers as the texts.

By itself, *selah* has remained a marginal word. Instrumental music has rarely been valued by the church and temple as much as the holy script.

In most worship services, folks gather to chat as the organist plays the prelude. The offering plates are passed to the sound of more instrumental music, often cut short when an impatient usher flicks a secret switch to ignite a bulb on the organ and notify the organist that the "essential" task is complete. Sadly, the instrumental postlude at the end of the service frequently devolves into "Go in peace; get out of my way!"

I have a high view of instrumental music as a potential spiritual gift for the listener and the musician alike. The *selah* work of a jazz quartet can utter things in the presence of God that mere words fail to say. A saxophone can lament on behalf of those who feel helpless. A piano may offer intercessions for those who are in need. A string bass can affirm the firm foundation of faith. Drums and cymbals may call pilgrims to break into joy.

Poet Ron Seitz has spoken about how, as a young man, he befriended writer and theologian Thomas Merton, who was then in his later years. Seitz tells of the night he went with Merton to a jazz club in Louisville. As the group began to play, Merton leaned over to whisper, "They're going to start talking to each other now. Listen." Then he moved closer to the bandstand to get a better look. Later, returning with his eyes wide, he said to Seitz, "Now that's praying. That's some kind of prayer! The new liturgy. Really, I'm not kidding."

SPEAKING OF PRAYER

What is prayer but the conversation of the soul addressed to God? Whether spoken aloud or silently, in a chorus of voices or in private, prayer is the respiration of the spiritual life. Like any conversation, it is two-sided, even if God's voice is spoken at a frequency we cannot hear. In that apparent silence, we are tempted to do all the talking. But spiritual directors encourage us to hush, to dwell in receptive silence. There is Holy Wisdom to receive.

Prayer is honest communication. Prayer aspires to tell the simple truth about what's going on within us and beyond us. It opens us to whatever God might do about our situation, prompts us to participate, and invites us to vulnerability and intimacy.

Prayer is the expression of a relationship. In prayer, we open our souls to the Presence greater than ourselves. We say thanks. We request help. We listen. As Charles Lloyd writes in the epigraph that begins this chapter, the prayers he offers consist of "asking the Creator for food." And the asking is done on the saxophone.

The Psalms of Israel help clarify and direct our prayer. A collection of 150 prayers in the center of the Bible, the Psalms cry and sing, beg and celebrate, interrogate and affirm. They voice our grief and wait for its healing. They declare surprising grace when it is discovered. They name the disconnections we experience and point toward holy restitution. They howl and dance and do everything in between. When we don't know what to say, the Psalms provide a vocabulary. And the "liner notes" suggest instrumentation. *Selah.*

When prayer becomes too selfish, the Psalms expand our spirits. When prayer hits a brick wall, the Psalms point beyond it. These poetic prayers provide focus and direction for the words we haven't yet found. They honestly voice our pain and point to God's justice. They release us, in the poetic phrase of jazz historian Albert Murray, to "the exorcism of despair."

And the psalms also return me to John Coltrane and *A Love Supreme* in all its power and raw emotion.

JAZZ, CONCEIVED IN PRAYER AND PRAISE

According to the mythology surrounding Coltrane's most famous recording, the composition was conceived in an extended time of reflection and meditation. One biographer describes how John sat cross-legged in a silk robe, meditating silently, seeking communion with the Almighty, when he was suddenly flooded with melodies from heaven. How this happened, exactly, the biographer did not describe, and Coltrane, in his modesty, would not disclose something so personal. What we do know is how Alice Coltrane, John's widow, later described this compositional experience to saxophonist Branford Marsalis:

> He went into isolation. We didn't see him; the children didn't know what was going on. I would take food up for him, but no one saw him for several days. So we said OK, we won't bother him, ask him any questions, or send notes or anything. About—I would imagine—a few days to a week, he came downstairs like Moses coming down from the mountain. And he said, "For the first time in my life, for the next album, I have all of the music. This is the first time that has ever happened to me."

John's typical pattern was to create music on the fly, to go into the recording studio with little preparation and then to trust the moment. However, *A Love Supreme* was preconceived, even as it was finished in the studio. And to this day, *A Love Supreme* remains one of the most studied and discussed compositions in all of jazz.

Later discovered by his family, the manuscript of Coltrane's original compositional "map" was given to the Smithsonian Institution's National Museum of American History. The guide reveals a suite in four movements, each in a different minor key, mapped out so that each member of Coltrane's quartet will have a prominent solo. The primary melodic motif is a four-note phrase, first played as a vamp by the bass and later chanted. "A love su-preme, a love su-preme" is the foundation of the whole piece, a proclamation that God's love is beneath our feet, above our heads, surrounding us on every side.

To reinforce the point, Coltrane concludes his solo on the first movement by playing the motif on his horn ("a love su-preme"), then continues to play the phrase in every key. The prominent Coltrane scholar Lewis Porter notes how unusual this is: "He's telling us that God is everywhere—in every register, in every key—and he's showing us that you have to discover religious belief. You can't just hit someone on the head by chanting right at the outset—the listener has to experience the process and then the listener is ready to hear the chant."

After this first movement, titled "Acknowledgement," a bass solo leads us into the next movement, "Resolution." John's band had been working on that melody in club gigs, but for the recording, it has been slightly reworked and put in a different key. The title echoes the testimony that he wrote for the album's liner, the only time Coltrane wrote such a piece. The text begins with a description of spiritual awakening. He then goes on to confess,

> As time and events moved on, a period of irresolution did prevail. I entered into a phase which was contradictory to the pledge and away from the esteemed path; but thankfully, now and again through the unerring and merciful hand of God, I do perceive and have been duly re-informed of His OMNIPOTENCE, and of our need for, and dependence on Him.

What listeners perceive in the recording and from Coltrane's notes is that he did not presume his faith journey was finished. Awakening required a reawakening, a "resolution" to begin anew. So when we meet the third movement, "Pursuance," a fast, explosive blues based on the "a love supreme" motif, we hear what some consider a musical narration of his journey of sanctification. Others, with the fury of the piece, surmise the artist is trying to outrun the temptations of the world. But all hear Coltrane climbing uphill with all the energy he can muster as he signals that the spiritual life requires energy, resilience, and perseverance to the end.

At the end of the suite, we hear the appropriately titled "Psalm." The pianist strikes an ominous C-minor chord and lets it shimmer for the next seven minutes. Above thundering tom-toms and a droning bass, Coltrane offers a long, melismatic melody unlike anything he had recorded to date. It rises and falls like a chant.

For years, the melody of "Psalm" was a mystery, only guided by John's cryptic description that it was "a musical narration of the theme." But biographer Lewis Porter reveals the confounding mystery's answer. Along with the rare liner notes that Coltrane composed for the album package, Coltrane included a long, free-verse poem entitled "A Love Supreme." It sounded like a meditation from the Bible's Psalms, rising and falling as breath, thanking God for grace, mercy, and peace. John names God as the Source ("all made in one") and Destination ("they all go back to God"), regularly punctuating with the refrain "Thank you, God." One day, as Dr. Porter listened to the fourth movement, he realized Coltrane was playing his "Psalm" on the tenor saxophone. His improvised melody, played this way only once, is a recitative of his poem of praise.

Other jazz scholars later confirmed what Trane had done. It appeared to be unprecedented. But in reality, Coltrane had done this before.

LAMENTING ON THE HORN

In November 1961, John Coltrane took his quartet for a week of live recordings at the Village Vanguard, a noted club in Greenwich Village. He titled one melody "Spiritual."

At first, "Spiritual" was considered a Coltrane composition. But later, it was revealed to be a tune John found in a book of African American spirituals collected by James Weldon Johnson. The source was the "older" version of the hymn "Nobody Knows the Trouble I've Seen." In Coltrane's imagination, the old hymn was transformed into a passionate cry lasting nearly fourteen minutes. A prayer in a minor key. In the liner notes, Coltrane wrote that he wanted to "get the original emotional essence of the spiritual."

Two years later, Coltrane recorded an original composition titled "Alabama," adding it to a live set recorded at the Birdland Jazz Club in New York. He did not tell his bandmates about the new tune when they recorded it on November 18, 1963. Nor did he reveal the title when he gave them the sparest of directions. Pianist McCoy Tyner began the performance the same way he would for the final movement of "A Love Supreme" a year later—with an ominous C-minor chord. Over that chord, John played a long melody unlike anything else he had ever composed. After a pause, the quartet began to improvise in steady time before returning to the melody.

When the title was finally revealed, the meaning of the composition began to come into focus. Two months prior to the recording date, at 10:22 a.m. on Sunday, September 15, white supremacist Robert Chambliss detonated fifteen sticks of dynamite that he and three other men had planted at Birmingham's Sixteenth Street Baptist Church. Four young girls, ages eleven to fourteen, were killed as they were putting on their choir robes in a basement restroom. They had just concluded a Sunday School lesson on the topic "The Love That Forgives." After he was arrested, Chambliss, a member of the Ku Klux Klan (KKK), was not convicted for the murders, only charged with the possession of dynamite.

The country was shaken by this act of domestic terrorism and the exoneration of the criminal act. The implicit threat from the KKK was that for those who were Black, there was no safety, not even in their own churches. The morning's Sunday School lesson was pushed toward incredulity. And although Coltrane never spoke publicly about the tragedy, one of his colleagues reported he was incensed. Not one to take a public stand on issues, John privately called the incident "reprehensible," particularly angry that it had happened in a house of God. The saxophonist kept his feelings to himself, maintaining his busy performance schedule and traveling widely. That is, until he recorded "Alabama."

The unusual melody floats like a chant. Clearly, it was composed, for the melody of the studio recording for the Birdland album is virtually identical to the version Coltrane and his quartet performed on a television show in San Francisco three weeks later.

Years later, McCoy Tyner said the tune was based on a speech by Martin Luther King Jr. More recently, scholars have suggested the melody originated in phrases from Dr. King's funeral eulogy for the young women murdered in the Birmingham blast. Phrases from Dr. King's speech can be clearly discerned in Coltrane's melody:

> So they did not die in vain.
> God still has a way of wringing good out from evil.
> The innocent blood of these little girls may well serve as a
>   redemptive force for this city.
> We must not despair. We must not become bitter.

Coltrane continues to pray through his horn. In his melody as well as his solo, his own intercessions arise for this broken world, for those who lost their children, for those wounded by the blast, and for those torn asunder by hatred and violence.

"Alabama" is a musical psalm of lament, voicing sorrow while shaking a fist toward heaven and demanding justice. It's little wonder that in recent years, in the days after George Floyd's murder beneath the knee of a white police officer, the jazz community revisited "Alabama"—as American society continues to confront the scars of systemic racism. In 2020, Ismail Muhammed wrote,

> When I listen to Coltrane playing over Tyner's piano, I hear smoke rising up from a smoldering crater, mingling with the voices of the dead. He asks us to peer down into the hole, to toss ourselves over into this absence . . .

> "Alabama" gives this unceasing immersion in grief a form. It's there in the song's disconcerting stops and starts, its disarticulated notes, its willingness to abandon virtuosity in favor of a style of playing that is repetitive, diffuse, tentative, and dissonant . . .

> Sometimes, you'd rather scream and storm than have to explain anything at all.

In another article, Colin Fleming wrote of the power he experienced in listening to "Alabama" anew: "It will wreck you. . . . [I]t's the sound of actual justice, a reminder to get to the other aspects of anger, to work one's way to the parts that can lead to reform.

A reminder of who we have it in us to be, and whom we might help. Which may well be the fundamental point of everything."

MUSIC AS PRAYER

When music finds us—or when the Holy finds us through music—it can speak *for* us. "I am praying through my fingers when I play," Mary Lou Williams said, "And when I get the good 'soul' sound, and I try to touch people's spirits." The honest and spiritually sensitive musician declares what others wish they could say if only they had the words—or notes. This is the power of "A Love Supreme," which prays out the spiritual life and announces we are surrounded by the supreme love of God.

The music can also speak *to* us, addressing brokenness, injustice, and hurt. And when it does, the musician becomes the prophet. By praying in the tonalities of lament, the musician names the disconnections between how it is and what it could be. Anger is voiced in the expectation that it will be addressed and remediated. Those with ears to hear are validated and empowered. Those who remain invested in the forces that demean and destroy are served notice that God is coming to make things right.

A passionate saxophone offers so much more than the soundtrack to a carefree life. Those with ears to hear can perceive a call to vision, a commitment to justice, and an invitation to all that is honest and true. John Coltrane understood this. After offering *A Love Supreme* as a gift of prayer, he noted, "Once you become aware of this force for unity in life, you can't forget it. It becomes part of everything you do. My goal in meditating on this through music however remains . . . to uplift people as much as I can. To inspire them to realize more and more their capacities for living meaningful lives."

IMPROVISATION: LATE-NIGHT THOUGHTS ON LISTENING TO COLTRANE'S *ASCENSION*

Coltrane beckons Trinity
with a triplet.
The prayer meeting is called to order
as seven horns confer
on the invocation.
Soon the band speaks
in tongues,
a brassy sassy sanctified cacophony.

As Coltrane steps forward to scream,
a voice floats in from the next room,
Turn that s*** down!
I will not oblige.
Privileged folk like me
have turned it down
far too long
while saxophonists need to
pray.

Who am I to mute another man's pain?
Let him speak,

let him cry,
let his broken words ascend
to where he can be heard and answered.

And should I listen in,
something in me can also be addressed.
Prayers don't merely ascend.
Sometimes prayers spin sideways.

CHAPTER NINE

BABEL AND BEBOP

The End Was in the Beginning

Bird gave the world his music and includes you. Besides, you can't steal a gift—if you can hear it, you can have it.

> —*Dizzy Gillespie to saxophonist Phil Woods*

Through our suffering God took pity on us and created the world's greatest true art: the "Negro Spirituals" and from the Spirituals: Jazz was born in all its creative and progressive forms.

> —*Mary Lou Williams*

WHO CREATED JAZZ?

Ferdinand "Jelly Roll" Morton was furious, his anger lingering even four months after he heard the radio broadcast for *Ripley's Believe It or Not!* In late March 1938, the nationally syndicated show featured W. C. Handy, the famous composer from Memphis. "Believe it or not," the show announced, Handy was the "father of jazz as well as the blues."

"You have done me a great injustice," Morton fumed in an open letter to the show. "It is evidently known, beyond contradiction, that New Orleans is the cradle of jazz, and I, myself, happened to be creator in the year 1902."

Those who knew Morton rolled their eyes. Jelly Roll was notoriously full of himself. That spring, he recorded about nine hours of music and interviews for the Library of Congress. Between the bawdy songs and tall tales from his Big Easy days, he insisted he alone was the creator of the music that had since left him behind.

In response to Morton's letter, W. C. Handy fired back days later from his publishing office in New York, reminding the world that his vocal quartet had performed at the Chicago World's Fair in 1893, traveling widely to present his compositions for concerts and minstrel shows. "Because of my exceptional ability to write down the things peculiar to (the African American culture)," he writes, "I created a new style of music which we now call the 'Blues' and no one contested in these twenty-five years my copyrights which I own." Regarding Morton, he concluded, "If he is as good as he says he is, he should have copyrighted and published his music so that he could not be running down deserving composers."

Who created jazz? Did it originate in New Orleans or Memphis?

Beneath the media squabble is a legitimate question about origins. The answers offer clues to where the music is headed—and what it demands of the spiritual life.

CRADLE, COTTON FIELD, AND CHURCH

Jelly Roll Morton was unquestionably the first great composer and orchestrator of the type of jazz he created in New Orleans—a genre that W. C. Handy had fashioned and popularized into the music we know as the blues. Each of these pioneers was a towering figure in the history of jazz, and both deserve recognition for the ways they shaped the music. But neither "created" jazz. The origins are as complicated and nuanced as any process of evolution, especially in a tradition that continues to develop.

Before Morton's claim that he composed the "King Porter Stomp" in 1906 (when he would have been sixteen), Scott Joplin itinerated through the Midwest as a pianist, giving a syncopated spin to music that drew its shape from marches. Joplin's first big tune, "Maple Leaf Rag," was published in 1899 as much for posterity as profit, for much of the music he created had not yet been written down. Soon, ragtime intoxicated the public—at a time when many American homes had a piano.

By the time Handy took his brass band on the road, the US military bands had demobilized at the end of the Spanish–American War in 1898. A port city like New Orleans had a glut of inexpensive used instruments and no shortage of those who wanted to play them. As theologian Harvey Cox points out, new Jim Crow policies in that city classified all people with "negro blood" as "colored." A wide variety of people—former slaves, Creoles of French and Spanish descent, dockworkers from the Caribbean, and others—were relocated into carefully designed "districts." And every district had its own brass band. The stage was set for a musical jambalaya to bubble up.

Prior to ragtime and the brass band, the music of the spirituals emerged through the southern American states, beginning as early as the late eighteenth century. Pious slaveowners, mostly Protestant, built churches for enslaved laborers to proclaim the Gospel and expected those enslaved to attend. They never anticipated, in the irony of grace, that some of those enslaved would begin to hear the Christian faith as an invitation to liberation. And that movement to liberation was evident in the music they created.

In church services, enslaved peoples heard the story of God saying, "Go down, Moses, way down in Egypt's land; tell old Pharoah, 'Let my people go!'" The old story now rang in a new song—a song that endured even after slaveowners saw fit to edit those verses out of their Bibles. Separated from family and familiar land, enslaved peoples could sing, "Sometimes I feel like a motherless child, a long way from home," never losing hope in returning. When the time was nigh, they could "steal away to Jesus," not merely as an emotional escape from their oppression but to share code language that declared when it was time to hit the Underground Railroad.

Forged in the language of faith, the spirituals pointed north in all kinds of ways. The minor-key melodies voiced their pain and suffering, frequently looking beyond, toward God's redemption. W. E. B. Du Bois named these the "Sorrow Songs." As he describes them in his classic treatise, *The Souls of Black Folk* (1903),

> Through all the sorrow of the Sorrow Songs there breathes a hope—a faith in the ultimate justice of things. The minor cadences of despair change often to triumph and calm confidence. Sometimes it is faith in life, sometimes a faith in death, sometimes assurance of boundless justice in some fair world beyond. But whichever it is, the meaning is always clear: that sometime, somewhere, (people) will judge (one another) by their souls and not by their skins.

W. C. Handy also spoke of the power of spirituals, long after the Civil War and the Emancipation Proclamation. "I think these spirituals did more for our emancipation than all the guns of the Civil War," he once said on the radio.

"The divine liberation of the oppressed from slavery is the central theological concept in the black spirituals," theologian James Cone explains. "These songs show that black slaves did not believe that human servitude was reconcilable with their African past and their knowledge of the Christian gospel."

Yet there may be one earlier source of jazz, preceding even the spirituals.

A CURIOUS JOURNEY

A few years ago, Willie Ruff, professor and jazz French hornist, took a break from his teaching responsibilities at Yale. He traveled to northern Alabama, where he had a home on generations of family land. New Haven, Connecticut, is known for many things, but catfish isn't one of them, so on Ruff's return to his hometown of Killen, Alabama, some authentic southern cuisine was at the top of his list.

Luckily, a neighbor told him about a little Presbyterian church that offered a dinner on the first and third Sundays in the summer. "You might have to listen to the choir and endure some preaching," said the neighbor, "but they serve the best catfish you've ever tasted."

As Ruff drew near the church, the music stopped him in his tracks. The choir was lining out the music just like the call-and-response singing of the Baptist churches from his childhood, a tradition he thought had died out. When the service was over, he made a beeline for the pastor—who was in a hurry to get some catfish for himself.

"Preacher," he said, "how come you Presbyterians are singing our Baptist songs?"

"Who said it's Baptist?" asked the pastor.

"Well," said Willie, "nobody said it was, but these are the songs that got us and our ancestors through the worst part of slavery."

The preacher shared how folks from the area were transplanted from many different areas. Maybe they had picked up the singing style while they had helped one another on the farms.

Willie replied, "But have you ever heard white people sing like this? There was a time, early in the days of slavery, when black and white all went to the same churches together. They weren't segregated until later."

"White Presbyterians sing like this?" said the pastor. "Why would they sing like this?"

"I don't know," said Willie, "but I know exactly how to find out. I work in an obscure little school up in Connecticut. They have a good divinity school and wonderful historians. I'm going to telephone them. I'll be back next Sunday, catfish or not."

His investigation led him to historians who said, "Yes, white Presbyterians did sing that way, but you're about a hundred and twenty-five years too late. But if you go to the Outer Hebrides islands of Scotland, it is rumored that they still sing this way. Not the hymns, only the Psalms, and only in their native tongue of Gaelic."

Willie flew to Scotland and made his way to Benbecula, a remote island in the Hebrides. In a congregation that sang in Gaelic, he was stunned to hear the same style of singing that he had encountered in the Mount Zion Cumberland Presbyterian Church in Killen, Alabama. His head was spinning. Which came first? The English or the Gaelic? Certainly, the Psalms preceded the spirituals. But how did all of this develop?

Then Willie recalled a time when he had performed with bebop superstar Dizzy Gillespie. Dizzy had quipped, "All my people spoke Gaelic." This offhand comment had struck Willie as a strange remark for the great-grandson of slaves from South Carolina! Now Willie was hooked.

Digging a little deeper, Willie researched immigration records that revealed a history of impoverished Gaels landing on the Carolina coast to begin a new life. And a feature associated with these populations is the double-decker church from plantation days, in which white folks sat below while their slaves sat unseen in the balcony.

It's not difficult to surmise what must have happened in some congregations. Those who sat on the balcony, stolen from Africa, heard Presbyterian sermons in Gaelic. The preaching left them confused—until they heard the psalm singing. The call-and-response musical tradition had always been strong in Africa, just as it had been with the Scots, who had begun lining out psalms before literacy was widespread. In the most unlikely way, these two cultures met musically—in church, of all places.

It seems we can conclude that the lined-out psalms preceded the spirituals that preceded jazz, at least in certain sections of the American south. There were ethnic differences, but the musical DNA was shared.

In short, jazz did not originate from a single source. It did not begin in a single location. The music has been a transcultural gumbo from the beginning, a bubbling stew of diverse ingredients. As someone once noted, rather than originate with a single flame, the music was ignited on a candelabra. The tradition developed organically, not academically. It has been transmitted by those who heard the melodies, imagined the harmonies, and passed it along with their own spin.

"The remarkable thing to me," concluded Willie Ruff after his research deep dive, "is that in the twenty-first century, the only people in the English-speaking world that are still doing call-and-response are the ones that are the most marginalized—the blacks here, and then these Gaels over in Scotland." They were singing the psalms—the original blues.

Marginalization and suffering, depth of emotion and spiritual power, call and response, the psalms. All common threads in the origins of jazz. All deeply human.

Who knows if this research will rewrite any history books? But it is fascinating to discover a new, unexpected ingredient bubbling in the gumbo pot. And to learn that Dizzy Gillespie's people really did speak Gaelic.

FROM BABEL TO PENTECOST

"Jazz is folk music," Keith Jarrett once told a Japanese interviewer. "Many people think that the world should speak the same language eventually. But I don't agree. If that was the way the earth was two hundred years ago, we would have no jazz."

Jarrett's insight into multiple languages casts an interesting light on the ancient Jewish story of the Tower of Babel. Found in the book of Genesis, the Babel story is a folk tale of a simpler, more uniform time in human history, recalling one human tribe, one language, and one set of vocabulary words. Perfect communication, right? Not necessarily.

The presumption of a human monoculture backfired. Whether an act of Divine judgment or inevitable humanity, one language exploded into many tongues. But what intrigues me is that Genesis offers this origin story as if to explain, "This is how we became who we are." The story of Babel suggests we were destined from the very beginning to speak in many languages.

Differences are a given. Diversity emerged in our origins, both human and musical. Variety is woven into our DNA. Something rich, powerful, and life-giving happens when these strands interweave, which has been going on ever since the beginning. And beneath it all, there has always been a strong connection to the Divine.

Ched Myers, biblical theologian and activist, points out jazz emerged at the same time as a radical event in the life of North American Christianity. In 1906, the same year Duke Ellington began piano lessons and Jelly Roll composed his greatest jazz tune, there was a spiritual earthquake in an alley of Los Angeles. A revival broke out on Azusa Street.

Secular news reports did not know how to describe what was happening. Myers quotes one newspaper describing the "disgraceful intermingling of the races, they cry and make howling noises all day and into the night. They run, jump, shake all over, shout to the top of their voice, spin in circles. . . . They claim to be filled with the spirit. They have a one-eyed, illiterate Negro as their preacher."

Today, the Azusa Street Revival is looked back on as the beginning of modern Pentecostalism. As Myers notes, William Seymour—the aforementioned "one-eyed" African American preacher—preached that the core message of Jesus was racial and gender equality. According to Seymour, all were equal in the heart of God. Every color line had been demolished by the cross of Christ. The Holy Spirit blew in the windows, igniting freedom, inspiring speech, and inviting all to claim their identity in a larger family than the one where they were born.

Revivals may burn hot for a while, like jazz performances, and then they fade. The Azusa Street Revival continued for a few years before it was corrupted by greed, internal power plays, and the reemergence of racist divisions. For a season, however, it revealed the fire of God's love for all. And it inspired pockets of widespread ecstatic spirituality unbound by social strata or physical appearances.

Such grace has always been threatening and subversive, especially in a world that dismisses those deemed different and crucifies those who spend time with the impure. Yet it reveals a truth that hard-edged fundamentalism and racist demands for purity cannot yet comprehend: In our differences, we were created to live together. To accept a diversity of human gifts. To overcome bigotry and inhabit a common humanity. To love one another.

And this is the work of the Holy, as Ched Myers understands it, "forever seeking to overcome oppression and domination in society, working through persons and social movements to bear witness to the possibilities of freedom and dignity. Jazz and church are cousins beneath the skin, and only when we get the family reunited will we experience healing and wholeness."

But, all that being said, we still haven't answered the question posed at the start of this chapter.

Jelly Roll Morton or W. C. Handy?

The truth is, the first great improviser in New Orleans was probably Charles "Buddy" Bolden, a churchgoing Baptist. When Buddy Bolden took out his cornet and blew variations on church hymns in New Orleans, it shook up a city already swimming in a multicultural pool. Buddy Bolden added his own hot sauce to the folk music of the people. It was swinging, scandalous, and completely alive. It was also influential. Louis Armstrong said he heard Buddy play when he was five years old; fifty years later, it left a vivid impression. Jelly Roll Morton declared the same, referring to Bolden as "King" and calling him "the most powerful trumpet in the world."

What's more, Willie Ruff remembers the day W. C. Handy visited his elementary-school classroom. Handy's hometown was across the Tennessee River from Ruff's. The blues master told the class of their shared musical heritage, along with all its diverse influences, especially the spirituals. "He was passionate about the music's worth," Willie recalls, "and admonished us children to always value all the rich legacy of our musical ancestry, the secular and the sacred alike."

No question about it. Jazz is born of diversity. As Keith Jarrett once said,

> I think jazz, no matter what we end up spending hours talking around the table with other so-called jazz experts, is . . . a mingling of cultures

in that music that's not existing anywhere else. It would be as if you were to write poetry in more than one language at a time and make it somehow into a coherent language of its own.

Jazz—the multilingual, cross-cultural, dynamic movement of the Spirit—offers a vision of human community. There was inclusion from the outset. The frozen chosen can be thawed, those wary of too much vitality are invited to dance, and the downtrodden are lifted up. This is the Holy Work of God. And it is the trajectory of the spiritual life.

IMPROVISATION: ANOTHER UNCLE

I have other sheep that do not belong to this fold. I must bring
them also.

—John 10:16

Well, that was a surprise!
Unknown to us,
Grandpa did not
stay home.
Long after he's gone
we discover we have
another uncle.

Nine birthed by his wife
were not enough.
Number Ten made
a round number.

Half of the originals
were gone before
the news leaked out.
We would never have known

had not Uncle 10
spit in a cup.

The news threatened
easy assumptions of purity
even though
mudbloods and mestizos
had long been grafted
to the Family Tree.

So the question bubbled
up again:
Dare we invite him to
the annual reunion?

Jazz sings,
let's give up on purity
and settle for welcome.
Everybody needs a family.
There's only one,
don't you know?

CHAPTER TEN

JAZZ AND OUR HIDDEN WOUND

Justice is what love looks like in public.

—*Dr. Cornel West*

Mr. Secretary, my job is to say to you, "Let justice roll down like mighty waters." Your job is to get the plumbing in place.

—*Rev. William Sloane Coffin, Jr. to Henry Kissinger*

AN UNCOMFORTABLE HONESTY

The message to bassist Charles Mingus was clear: "You cannot include *those* lyrics on this recording."

Mingus was in 30th Street Studio, a decommissioned Presbyterian Church in Manhattan newly transformed into a world-class recording studio. He had gathered his band to record *Mingus Ah Um*, the album that would become his masterwork, featuring musical tributes Charles wrote to honor saxophonists Lester Young and Charlie Parker, pianist Jelly Roll Morton, and bandleader Duke Ellington.

The album also included "Fables of Faubus," a song dedicated to Orval E. Faubus, the governor of Arkansas. It was not a tribute. Over three years after the US Supreme Court's decision to desegregate public schools, Faubus had stalled action to do so before openly defying the order. Nine African American students were scheduled to attend Central High School in Little Rock at the beginning of the 1957 school year. Faubus ordered the Arkansas National Guard to prevent it. It was an inflammatory conflict played out on the national stage, exposing the deep resentment of all who opposed the growing civil rights movement. After a twenty-day conflict, President Dwight Eisenhower invoked the Insurrection Act of 1807, calling on troops to enforce the federal law. The students were protected by the soldiers and admitted into the high school, where they were verbally abused by their classmates.

To mark the shameful event, Charles Mingus wrote "Fables of Faubus" with a rhythm that swaggers and a harmony that is mournful like a spiritual. At points, the melody is childish—and then it dawns on listeners that what they are hearing is a parody. Mingus is ridiculing Faubus for his bigotry.

As if that message were not clear enough, the band created song lyrics on the bandstand as they developed the music. Charles sang the words, punctuated by drummer Danny Richmond's refrains. Framing the lyric as a prayer, they begged God to protect them from shooting, stabbing, and tar-and-feathering. They begged the Almighty to eliminate the KKK and the Nazi swastika. And they denounced the governor as a "sick fool," rhyming his name with "ridiculous."

The business executives for the recording label said, "We can't let you put those words on a record!" Columbia Records was a big company with a national distribution network. They feared the message was too inflammatory, particularly for southern customers. The inevitable controversy would destroy sales of an otherwise stellar instrumental recording, so Columbia refused to allow Mingus to sing or print the lyrics on *Mingus Ah Um*.

It was a disappointing decision for the musician, but the very next year, Mingus recorded the song for another record label, lyrics and all. The song title was changed to "Original Faubus Fables," and the message was loud and clear. In the words of one jazz critic, the unexpurgated version was "a classic Negro put-down in which satire becomes a deadly rapier-thrust. Faubus emerges in a glare of ridicule as a mock villain whom no one really takes seriously. This kind of commentary, brimful of feeling, bitingly direct and harshly satiric, appears far too rarely in jazz."

Indeed.

The recording business has always been a business, not a prophetic denunciation of bigotry and injustice. Financial self-interest has a way of squelching honesty. Racial satire appears rarely, even when those who have been oppressed find their voice in the wider public.

Mingus, ever the provocateur, wasn't holding back. He continued to perform the song through the 1960s, expanding the performance sometimes to thirty minutes. On occasion, he inserted musical quotes of the Confederate anthem, "Dixie," in making his point.

"I have to do it," he was telling us through his music. "I have to tell the truth."

YOU CANNOT HANDLE THE TRUTH

One night in 1939, singer Billie Holiday introduced a new song at the Café Society, the first racially integrated nightclub in America. Written by the teacher Abel Meeropol under a pseudonym, the song "Strange Fruit" offered a shocking description of the lynching of African Americans as "strange fruit hanging from the poplar trees." Meeropol wrote the words after having seen a disturbing photograph of two Black men hung from a tree by a mob in Indiana. Originally conceived as a poem, "Strange Fruit" was written in protest of this barbaric form of social control.

Accounts differ as to how the poem became a song, but nobody disputes the impact the song had on audiences when Billie Holiday sang it. It became her signature song.

The manager of the Café Society determined a set of rules regarding how "Strange Fruit" would be performed in the club. It would be the last song of the evening to maximize its impact. The wait staff would stop serving food and drink. All lights in the room would be cut except for a single spotlight on Billie. She sang it with eyes closed, as if offering a lament. The crowd would sit in stunned darkness, left to ponder the scene described by the song. To nobody's surprise, Columbia Records, her recording company, refused to record it. They did, however, grant her a one-session release so she could sing it for another record label.

"Strange Fruit" stunned everybody who heard it. As theologian James Cone observes, it exposed the hypocrisy of Christianity as practiced in parts of white America. A faith that began with the atrocity of Jesus hung "on a tree" was the faith of many who looked away—or jeered—when African Americans were hung on trees.

"Billie Holiday's rendition of 'Strange Fruit,'" Dr. Cone wrote, "forced white listeners to wrestle with the violent truth of white supremacy." As an early call for civil rights, it empowered those who heard its proclamation of the bitter truth.

Yet as much as "Strange Fruit" empowered the desire for justice, it also enraged many white listeners. As that haunting song created ripples across the land, it infuriated the likes of Harry Anslinger, head of the Federal Bureau of Narcotics. The internal memos he wrote from his office about Black musicians reeked of racism. He hated jazz and despised the rebellious people who made it. Unable to use his office to clear the streets of all jazz musicians, he turned his singular gaze on Billie. There were rumors, all true, that she had a heroin addiction. Anslinger determined the best way to silence that song was to bust her for drugs. An agent was sent to infiltrate her circle. All the time, she kept singing "Strange Fruit."

Billie was arrested, sent to prison for a year, and released. She began to sing again, and Anslinger went after her once more. Even though there were many other high-profile addicts in the entertainment industry, some of them white, Holiday was his Public Enemy Number One. She was Black, female, a jazz singer, and she would not stop singing that song about whites lynching Black bodies.

His acts of cruelty reached further lows when she became deathly ill from cirrhosis of the liver, complicated by cardiac issues. Anslinger sent narcotics agents to her hospital room, where they "found" a small packet of heroin six feet from her bed, a distance she would have been incapable of reaching in her state. As she lay critically ill, he had them arrest her, stationing two police officers outside her door to keep her in and to keep others out. For a month, Holiday struggled for her life, suffering the effects of withdrawal, until she could fight no more. On July 17, 1959, she died, handcuffed to her hospital bed.

Still, the song that sounded the truth of lynchings played on. Forty years later, *Time Magazine* would name "Strange Fruit" the best song of the century. Holiday's original recording sold over one million copies and was posthumously inducted into the Grammy Hall of Fame.

Beyond every attempt to suppress it, the song grew in power. Why? Because it told the truth.

LIVING IN THE LIGHT

Those who espouse the spiritual life understand it confronts the uncomfortable truth about us, our desire for power, and the ways we continue to mistreat one another.

The twofold call to love God and one's neighbor is easier to say than to do. But when the Bible uses the verb *love*, it expresses an active engagement for the benefit of those we are called to love. Love works in the best interest of others. To love God is to "keep the commandments," which benefit all people. Surely this compels the spiritual person to love the neighbor in tangible and humanitarian ways.

Honest love also exposes the sham of so-called religion. Eight hundred years before Jesus, the prophet Amos spoke in a time of national peace and prosperity. His words blasted through the superficial spiritual practices of his day. The prophet caricatures religion as merely going through the motions while ignoring God and plundering neighbors.

So the prophet Amos records the words he hears God, the Creator of all, speak:

> I hate, I despise your festivals,
>
> > and I take no delight in your solemn assemblies.
> Even though you offer me your burnt offerings and grain
> > offerings,
> > I will not accept them;
> and the offerings of well-being of your fatted animals
> > I will not look upon.
> Take away from me the noise of your songs;
> > I will not listen to the melody of your harps.
> But let justice roll down like waters,
>
> > and righteousness like an ever-flowing stream.

The prophet's concern was for truth-telling, for justice, defined as fairness enacted for every person under heaven. As Dr. Cornel West is often quoted as saying, "Justice is what love looks like in public." Justice begins with the affirmation that all of us belong to the one human family. It lives and breathes with authentic hospitality. It exudes equity and equality. Justice pursues the public good and repairs what selfishness has twisted out of shape.

As we have seen, jazz was born from mixed parentage and continues to point toward inclusion. Grown from the soil of oppression, jazz promises to break free of its chains and declare freedom. If justice rolls down like waters, a spiritual life shaped by jazz will work out the plumbing. It will lift those who have been put down. As trumpeter Wynton Marsalis said in an onstage conversation about race at the Chautauqua Institution, "Instead of you asking when I'm going to get up, try to help me up." It is a decision between having agency over others or helping them.

A TOUGH NIGHT IN EAST CAROLINA

The college crowd was stomping its feet, waiting for the concert to begin. East Carolina College in Greenville, North Carolina, was hosting the renowned Dave Brubeck Quartet.

This was the last US show before Brubeck's band would leave for a three-month international tour. Sponsored by the State Department in early 1958, Dave and his musicians were sent as ambassadors of democracy to Poland, Turkey, India, Ceylon (modern-day Sri Lanka), Pakistan, Iran, and Iraq. The State Department hoped to influence nations teetering toward totalitarianism by sending a jazz group that modeled freedom. It was an attempt to thaw the Cold War by sending a group of cool jazz musicians.

But before their travels, at East Carolina College, the Dave Brubeck Quartet was informed they would not be allowed to go on stage. Why? Because the quartet had a Black bass player.

It was Eugene Wright's first week with the band. An African American bassist with hard-swinging credentials, he could lay down the beat as drummer Joe Morello built layers of elaborate rhythms. Wright was the perfect addition to the band and essential for the way Dave wanted to develop the music.

Because he was new to the group, Wright had not yet posed for any of the quartet's publicity photos, and nobody had seen the need to notify the college administration of the change in personnel. When the quartet rolled into Greenville, however, the dean of student affairs declared that Jim Crow laws outlawed the performance of an interracial group, so the Brubeck group could not perform with its bass player.

While Dave argued with him, somebody in the crowd got wind of the impasse. The students began to chant Eugene's name and stomp their feet. Frustrated, the dean called the college president, who tried to convince Brubeck to change his mind. Dave countered, "Tomorrow, I'm taking my band to play behind the Iron Curtain, and you're telling us that we can't play in our own country?"

The impasse went on for over an hour as the college president contacted the governor of North Carolina. "Better let them play," the governor replied. "We don't want another Little Rock." With this, the college president consented, saying to Brubeck, "You can go on, as long as you keep Mr. Wright in the background where he can't be seen too well."

Brubeck did not comment. He turned to tell the band about the situation. Then he said to his bass player, "They have turned off the microphone on the bass, but I have a microphone for making announcements. I want you to come out front and use my mic when it's time for you to play your solo." Wright did just that, and the audience went crazy. The crowd stood and cheered. As Dave would later recall, "We integrated the university that night."

But beyond the university, the agitation was clear. After the show, the band needed a protective escort from the state police just to get out of town. And this was not an isolated incident. The integrated Dave Brubeck Quartet would face trouble again. Not in their overseas travel but in America.

After returning from the State Department tour, where they played eighty concerts in fourteen countries, Dave recorded *Jazz Impressions of Eurasia*, a collection of original tunes inspired by the tour. He went on to record *Time Out*, his most famous album, in 1959. It featured "Blue Rondo a la Turk," based on a rhythm he heard in Istanbul, and Paul Desmond's tune "Take Five." Record sales soared, Brubeck's popularity blew through the roof, and his quartet worked all the time.

Later that year, Dave's booking agency planned to capitalize on his success. The agency put together a concert tour of twenty-five universities, all located in the southern United States. The financial package was enticing, equivalent to $400,000 in today's currency—an astronomical sum for a jazz group. There was just one catch: Brubeck had to replace Eugene Wright with a white bass player. He refused. This led to a showdown with his agent, Joe Glaser. When the dust settled, twenty-three of the twenty-five dates were canceled. For Dave, it was a matter of principle.

It would not be the last challenge. A student-initiated concert at the University of Georgia was nixed by the college administration. The KKK tried to stop a Brubeck concert in Alabama. One venue after another attempted to book Wright in separate hotels, removed from the three white musicians, but Brubeck refused to allow it.

In what would have been the band's greatest public exposure to date, the Bell Telephone Hour booked the Brubeck Quartet to perform on national television. When the band arrived for the broadcast, Dave discovered the producers wanted his bass player to perform behind a curtain, where he could not be seen. After debating this to no avail, Dave turned to the band and said, "Come on, guys. We're going to go." They walked out of the NBC studio without playing a note. A long while later, he reflected on the decision in conversation with me. "We did the right thing," Dave told me. "There are a lot of things more important than money."

EXPOSING THE WOUND

Wendell Berry, the southern farmer and essayist, has written of the injustice of racism as America's "hidden wound," citing how, throughout history, it has been damaging to slave and master alike in an injury that lingers in those still recovering from the deep stain of slavery. It is less obvious, but no less real, he says, in those who cannot address their own complicity in the caste system that has privileged those with white skin at the expense of others.

What makes Dave Brubeck remarkable is his clear-eyed, open-hearted courage. This level of respect for others and the courage to act on it was developed during his upbringing and continued into his adult life. Born in 1920, Brubeck was the third son of a classical pianist mother and a rough-and-tumble cattle rancher father, which Brubeck referred to as an unlikely marriage.

Dave's two older brothers followed their mother and went into music. Pete Brubeck thought his son Dave should go out into the fields with him, so Dave went to college to become a veterinarian.

However, he kept sneaking across the campus to play the pianos in the conservatory. Finally, one of his zoology professors said, "Brubeck, your mind's not here. It's across the lawn in the conservatory. Please go there. Stop wasting my time and yours."

After graduating from the College of the Pacific in Stockton, California, he joined the army during World War II and was shipped off to Europe. The war marked the beginning of his many globetrotting adventures, pushing him beyond the provincialism of northern California. It also sparked the crisis of faith mentioned in chapter 4 and brought him to the question "Did God create every person or not? If so, why can't we live together as one family?"

These recurring questions would prompt him to build friendships across racial and cultural boundaries. He formed an interracial jazz band when serving in General Patton's army during the war, befriending musicians who could play well, which introduced him to musicians of color. After the war, he returned home to a country filled with the same racial divisions as when he'd left.

As he reflected on this experience in Ken Burns's monumental documentary on jazz, he recalled a powerful moment from his teenage years. One day, while riding on the cattle range, his father took him down to the Sacramento River. They met a Black rodeo rider, and Pete said, "Open your shirt for Dave and show him your chest." The man did so, revealing a cattle brand on his chest.

Pete Brubeck said, "Something like this should never happen again."

This was a foundational moment that would shape the trajectory of Dave's career. It moved him so much that, decades later, he broke into tears when describing the scene to the filmmaker Ken Burns. After the film crew departed from his home, he confided to his son Chris that he "blew it." He thought he should have kept a stiffer lip and not gotten so emotional on camera. But Burns later told Chris that the story was the emotional centerpiece of the whole nineteen-hour documentary.

If jazz can shape our spiritual lives, if it can teach us to love our neighbors, it will also invite us into the work of telling the truth, expose the wounds of injustice, and encourage us to create a just and hospitable society for all. Jazz, like the spiritual life, requires a fearless posture of openness. As with the musicians we see who, at great personal cost, opened the doors to truth, we meet the invitation to be open to the moment, to the occasion, and to those around us.

CLARITY AND COMMITMENT

This openness to the moment certainly bubbled up in Brubeck's music. Repeatedly in his life and music, there are examples of how his clarity and courage became commitments. The following are just a few examples.

Dave created a musical with his wife, Iola, called *The Real Ambassadors*, based on Brubeck's experiences as a cultural ambassador for the State Department. It played only once, at the 1962 Monterey Jazz Festival, but it served as a platform to wrestle with the civil rights issues that were gripping the nation.

Dave composed the music, and his wife wrote the lyrics. They invited no less a figure than Louis Armstrong to have a starring role. This would be their only public collaboration with Armstrong, who was deeply moved by the opportunity to tell the truth about his own struggles with racism.

One of the featured cuts begins with the vocal trio Lambert, Hendricks, and Ross. They sang a churchlike chant behind Armstrong. Over that backdrop, Louis sings,

They say I look like God. Could God be black? My God!
If all are made in the image of thee, could thou perchance a
   zebra be?

He's watchin' all the Earth. He's watched us from our birth.
And if He cared if you black or white, he'd a mixed one
   color, one just right.
Black or white. One just right.

The year was 1961, and America was not ready to embrace such lyrics. The Brubecks had hoped to put the show on Broadway but never found the funding. The production folded. As with "Fables of Faubus" and "Strange Fruit," the show was simply too truthful for its time.

As the tumultuous decade of the 1960s unfolded, Dave began to write sacred oratorios. His first major piece was called *The Light in the Wilderness*, a choral and orchestral setting of the teachings of Jesus, including the Sermon on the Mount. Created in 1967 as Dave broke up his quartet, it was performed and recorded with the Cincinnati Symphony Orchestra.

After the piece premiered, a Jewish rabbi named Charles Mintz contacted Brubeck and asked, "Why don't you create a piece based on the Jewish scriptures?" After consulting three rabbis, Brubeck put together a major piece called *The Gates of Justice*, a fascinating work drawing from the Psalms and prophetic texts about justice and the words of Dr. Martin Luther King Jr., who had just been assassinated. Dave dug in deeply, writing in his program notes,

> Because of their long history of suffering, Jews and American blacks know better than any other people the consequences of hate and alienation. It is impossible to concern oneself with the history and tradition of either without feeling overwhelmed by the inequities and injustices that have pervaded all strata of society. The spiritual and emotional ties, born of suffering, which bind these people together, have much to teach all of us on this shrinking planet. It is the strength of such moral fiber that will be our ultimate salvation.

In the middle of the oratorio, Brubeck dusted off an earlier composition called "Lord, Lord." It was a bluesy lament, like many of the Jewish psalms. The opening lines sing, "Lord, Lord, what will tomorrow bring? Today I felt an arrow stinging in a wound so deep, my eyes refuse to weep. What will tomorrow bring?"

In the middle of the choral version, Dave makes a stunning decision as composer. He inserts a series of racial epithets, shouted by the choir. Juxtaposed by the lament, they jolt us to ask the question that Dave asks, "When are we going to get away from this kind of condemnation of each other?"

The last example I'll share of Dave's courage and openness is one I experienced when I met Mr. Brubeck in 1998. Thanks to my beloved grandmother's influence, I fell under his musical spell when I was a teenager. But I never expected the phone to ring years later and a pleasant voice to ask me to take part in a special weekend in Princeton, New Jersey.

Sue Ellen Page, choir director at Nassau Presbyterian Church, had a musical dream. She had assembled an interracial children's choir from Princeton and Trenton, two widely disparate communities. Having previously presented programs on peace, Sue Ellen wanted them to now sing about justice. She decided to commission Dave Brubeck to create a large choral work based on a poem by Langston Hughes.

Sue Ellen hoped that Dave would use this poem as a springboard for collecting many biblical texts that could also be included and developed in the work. She marked the poem in a volume of collected works by Hughes and sent it off to Brubeck's home in Connecticut. However, Dave misunderstood the assignment and composed settings for nineteen Hughes poems for the children's choir. He was embarrassed to discover his mistake and offered to return the commission money.

Sue Ellen looked over his work and said, "No, keep going! You have created something enduring, and it must be sung."

One day, Rev. Clarence Ammons, the pastor of Nassau Church and Sue Ellen's colleague, called me to say, "We are bringing Dave Brubeck and his quartet to play in our church for a weekend in October. Would you be available to preach a sermon? It's the weekend of the premiere of the Brubeck setting of Hughes poems."

"Yes!" Quickest decision I have ever made.

That was the genesis of my friendship with Dave, which lasted for the last fourteen years of the master's life.

The center of that unreleased work was Brubeck's setting of a Langston Hughes poem entitled "I Dream a World." Hughes imagined a world of mutual respect, filled with love and peace, untainted by greed or cruelty. All would share in the earth's resources. Every person would be free, regardless of worldly category.

Hughes's poem voiced the vision that Dave Brubeck dreamed into reality, and the poem held a deep significance for him. After Dave passed away, his wife, Iola, stood in the pulpit of the Cathedral of St. John the Divine in New York and read it for the crowd that gathered for his memorial service in 2013. For a moment, those of us who were there could taste the dream for ourselves.

Perhaps Wynton Marsalis summed it up best. When his Lincoln Center Jazz Orchestra presented a tribute concert of Dave's music, Wynton said, "He's important because he stood up for civil rights when many of us sat down."

How appropriate those words are for music that is shaped by the values of community, for a person whose values reflected the embodiment of a jazz-shaped spiritual life.

IMPROVISATION: HELL-BENT

The Brubecks wrote:

"They say
I look like God."
Only if you do, too.
Every soul bleeds
the same color.

Yet why do we
pierce one another?
It is the ancient enigma
of the torn heart,
created for peace,
hell-bent on pain,
especially if it lifts
me
while I kneel on
the neck of
Brother or Sister.

They say
you look like God.

How difficult to
claim truth
if I will not
believe there is
space for both of
us.

Fortunately,
I shall not
have the last
word on the
matter.

God knows.

CHAPTER ELEVEN

THE HANG
Grooving in Community

A jazz band means that we hear a collective art in which there is never anything like a "solo" unless one is playing alone. Otherwise it is always a group effort in which each member of the ensemble has chosen to help everyone else sound good. Help is the essential aspect of the art. The grandeur of the music arrives through that process.

—*critic Stanley Crouch*

What's a good gig? I ask three questions. Is the music happening? Is the bread happening? Is the "hang" happening? Two out of three is a good gig.

—*pianist Bill Mays*

POSING FOR *ESQUIRE* MAGAZINE

The editorial office thought it sounded like a great idea. There would be an all-jazz issue of *Esquire* magazine, and it would include a photograph with as many jazz musicians as possible. It was the summer of 1958, and the photo was the brainchild of Art Kane, the brand-new art director of the magazine.

Art wasn't an experienced photographer and didn't have a studio, but he had a vision. The photo would be a two-page spread shot in Harlem, as close to the center of the jazz community as anybody could find. He put out the word, "If you want to get your picture in *Esquire*, show up at 17 E. 126 Street at 10:00 a.m. on August 12, 1958."

Art did not realize that 10:00 a.m. was a nearly impossible time to gather musicians who performed into the wee hours of the morning. As one band member quipped, "For most of us, 10:00 comes only once a day." Yet fifty-eight musicians showed up, along with a dozen curious kids from the neighborhood.

That was when the chaos began.

Kane stood on the steps of the brownstone across the street, yelling in vain as he attempted to direct the scene. The musicians ignored him, hugging, slapping each other on the backs, and exclaiming, "How ya doing, baby?" It was a joyful reunion at an unlikely hour. Usually a scattered community, these musicians were glad to be all be united on those stairs. They wanted to catch up with one another, not merely pose for a picture.

Eventually, Kane gave up trying to manage the scene and started taking shots with his camera, hoping one would turn out well. Count Basie got tired of standing and sat on the curb, and one of the neighborhood kids started playing with his hat. Willie "The Lion" Smith also decided to sit and didn't appear in the final photo. Thelonious Monk, always wanting to stand out in a crowd, figured his colleagues would wear dark suits, so he showed up in a lightly colored jacket and stood in the front row next to two women of the jazz scene, Marian McPartland and Mary Lou Williams. Dizzy Gillespie stuck out his tongue at fellow trumpeter Roy Eldridge.

On its release in the January 1959 issue of *Esquire*, the photograph was dubbed "A Great Day in Harlem." Even though most of the musicians in the photo have by now passed away, it has been reprinted countless times and remains a visual reminder that jazz has always been a communal art form.

GREATER THAN THE SUM OF THE PARTS

In the "glory days" of the mid-twentieth century, big bands often traveled together on buses, working strings of one-nighters, eating on the fly, catching sleep when they could. Sometimes the performances were hundreds of miles apart. As Benny Goodman once remarked, "There are more towns in America that I have only seen after dark than I care to think about."

Bass player Tony Marino once remarked after a big concert in Paris with a well-known vocalist, "Didn't see it. We landed at the airport, checked into the hotel, put on the tuxedos, caught the van to the venue, and played the concert. After that, the van returned us to the hotel. The manager said we would leave for the airport at 3:30 a.m. to fly home. Never saw Paris." He paused and added, "I think I saw the Eiffel Tower when the plane took off."

For many jazz musicians, this peripatetic lifestyle can lead to loneliness and any number of bad habits. To counter this, musicians often make most of the opportunities to spend time together whenever they can. Sometimes this happens musically in jam sessions. Or it can happen afterward with *the hang*, as musicians extend the time together, hanging out. Whether it's a long dinner after a concert or hilarious stories told over a shared bottle of wine, the fellowship is the antidote to isolation.

Making jazz fosters comradery. Maybe it's the shared creativity. Or the mutual synchronization of rhythms. Maybe it's the unleashing of emotions. Perhaps all the above, but something deep also emerges from teamwork—which is the essence of jazz as a musical form.

Imagine, for instance, a jazz quartet of saxophone, piano, bass, and drums. They play together, and everybody assumes a role. The bass player provides a swinging foundation, establishing the pulse and hinting at the harmony. The drummer keeps the fire stoked, reinforcing the rhythm and provoking others to engage in dialogue. A pianist joins the conversation by adding well-punctuated chords. The saxophonist states the melody, strongly supported by all others. At

THRIVING ON A RIFF

any moment, the musicians might switch roles, especially if they are listening to one another, choosing to receive the gifts that the other musicians bring, and daring to contribute to the musical dialogue.

In his autobiography, jazz great Miles Davis wrote,

> That was my gift, you know, having the ability to put certain guys together that would create a chemistry and then letting them go; letting them play what they knew, and above it. I didn't know exactly what they would sound like together when I first hooked up guys. But I think it's important to pick intelligent musicians because if they're intelligent and creative then the music can really fly.

Jazz is a rare form of group art. The poet composes in solitude. Painters and sculptors work in isolation. Yet most jazz is created in the community. The music is inherently collaborative, leading to collegiality. Within a jazz group, each musician brings their ability. When the group is working together, the sum is greater than the parts.

In his study of improvisation, musician Stephen Nachmanovitch describes the benefits that come from a group of creative people working together: "Shared art-making is, in and of itself, the expression of, the vehicle for, and the stimulus to human relationships. The players, in and by their play, build their own society. As a direct relationship between people, unmediated by anything other than their imaginations, group improvisation can be a catalyst to powerful and unique friendships."

Nachmanovitch compares it with the phenomenon called *entrainment*, the occasion when two or more different rhythms become a single pulse. Say, for instance, several construction workers are hammering shingles on a roof. After a few minutes, their various poundings will fall into the same rhythm. They don't need to talk about it beforehand; it just happens.

The singer Anita O'Day took it even further: "I can tell you now that musical intimacy is on a completely different plane—deeper, longer-lasting, better than the steamiest sexual liaison. Passion wears out, but the closer you work with a really rhythmical, inventive swinging musician, the closer you become."

IN THE ECONOMY OF GRACE

In the economy of grace, reminiscent of the jazz community, there is shared clarity of purpose and creative use of collective gifts. The apostle Paul reminds us that everybody has something to offer. We are not complete in ourselves. We exist to help and encourage one another. You can almost hear Paul's words in Nachmanovich's words earlier—almost even hear the music as Paul writes, "God has so arranged the body, giving the greater honor to the inferior member, that there may be no dissension within the body, but the members may have the same care for one another. If one member suffers, all suffer together with it; if one member is honored, all rejoice together with it."

Some of us will quickly recall groups of people we know in our families, offices, and churches. But in my case, I tend to think in terms of music and the Duke Ellington orchestra.

Ellington, perhaps the most prolific composer in American history, did not merely write tunes. He created music that played to the strengths of the individual musicians in his band. If trumpeter James "Bubber" Miley played with creative flair with a mute made from a toilet plunger, Duke wrote it into his music. If Johnny Hodges had a certain way of sliding up to his notes, Duke expected him to do the same with his melodies. In other words, Ellington's genius was his ability to bring a community of musicians together. Sure, he played the piano, but he frequently quipped that his main instrument was the orchestra. In his group, the drummer could not say to the bass player, "I have no need of you." Neither could the saxophonist say to the trombonist, "You don't belong up here." They relied on one another.

When people in a group trust one another, they reap extraordinary benefits. As Stephen Nachmanovitch observes, "Beyond the aesthetic surprises we can find in our own exploration of our craft, we join in community with others and respond to each other, thanks to the power of listening, watching, sensing. The shared reality we create brings up even more surprises than our individual work."

THE TEEN WHO BECAME A SHEPHERD

On a Monday night in August 1934, a young teenager listened to a new kind of music. He stood transfixed, certain he had never heard music like that before and surely not in the small town of Berwick, Pennsylvania. Juan had traveled about a half hour from his uncle's home, where he lived, and shelled out ninety-nine cents for tickets at the West Side Park dance hall, where Duke Ellington and His Famous Orchestra were playing.

Ellington had developed his orchestra during a three-and-a-half-year stint as the house band for Harlem's Cotton Club. They provided music for stage shows, which included singing, dancing, and instrumental features. Duke used his residency as a composer's workshop, creating over one hundred tunes during that time. Radio broadcasts brought him national recognition, and recordings extended his reach even further. In the middle of 1931, the Ellington band departed the Cotton Club to go on the road—a set of tours that would keep them crisscrossing the country and the world for the next thirty years.

By the time Ellington and his band played in Berwick, they were a well-oiled machine. And standing in front of the band the entire night was Juan Garcia Velez.

Juan couldn't stop tapping his feet. Born in Puerto Rico, his impoverished parents had sent him to live in Pennsylvania with his aunt and uncle. Under their strong influence, he attended their Lutheran church and with their help would later go on to study at Susquehanna University and attend Gettysburg Seminary. By the time he met his wife, Audrey, he had adopted his aunt's last name, Gensel, as his own. Later, ordained as a Lutheran pastor, he served as a chaplain in World War II, returning to the States to serve two congregations in Ohio. But he would never forget that night, as a teenager, when he fell under Ellington's spell.

When he took a ministerial position at Advent Lutheran Church in New York City, Juan—who began calling himself John—began to visit the local jazz clubs. Soon it became his passion. Intrigued by the music, he decided to learn more. He enrolled in a college course on

"The Influence of Jazz on Modern Culture," taught by music critic Marshall Stearns. His class assignment was to go out to clubs and listen to more jazz. The course ended, but he didn't stop going to the clubs, often several times a week. Before long, Rev. John Garcia Gensel had become a regular on the jazz scene.

One night, one of the musicians John was watching asked if they could meet to discuss some personal problems. The word began to spread whenever the "jazz priest" was in the house, and Gensel gained the trust and friendship of scores of musicians, listening with an open heart, free from judgment. He took the music and the musicians seriously.

The Lutheran bishop took notice as Rev. Gensel built relationships with the musicians and reassigned him to a new position on the staff of Saint Peter's Lutheran Church in New York: pastor to the jazz community. In that role, he performed musicians' marriages, baptized their children, and memorialized those who departed. Thanks to John's influence, Saint Peter's became known as the jazz church, a safe place for creative souls.

In 1965, John established a weekly jazz vespers at the church, inviting the city's musicians to blend his traditional Lutheran worship with the creative fire of their improvisation. The weekly vespers service continues to this day, held late in the afternoon on Sundays, to benefit those for whom ten o'clock comes only once a day.

Out of the scores of musicians the jazz pastor befriended, John built a special bond with Duke Ellington, whom he met after moving to New York. It was a mutual friendship. Ellington asked for counsel, and Gensel encouraged the master to compose music with religious themes. Duke took it one step further, dedicating a new composition in John's honor. He called it "The Shepherd to the Night Flock" and performed it regularly in a series of sacred jazz concerts.

As Ellington wrote in his autobiography,

Pastor Gensel often went without, denying the needs of his own family, and even using money earned by his beautiful wife as a schoolteacher in order to pay the rent, or doctor's bills, or to buy food for some of the less fortunate night people. . . . His is pure humanism and the type of true unselfishness that mark a man as a true representative of God.

"Rev. Gensel was the easiest man in the world to talk with," one musician told me. "No pretension, no holier-than-thou condescension, and completely available to anybody who needed him. He knew how to hang out with us. Everybody needs a friend like that."

FRIENDSHIP IS ANOTHER WORD FOR LOVE

The hang has long served many purposes. It is a way for wandering musicians to stay connected. It offers an informal academy for learning the tricks of the musical trade from one another, provides a network for sharing news and passing along tips for getting gigs, and offers a way to reduce stress and offer emotional support. But the greatest gift it provides is friendship—deep and good-humored expressions of humanity. There is something deeply spiritual about friendship.

After a recent jazz concert, my wife and I were invited to join the musicians for dinner. It was a Sunday-afternoon tribute to the music of Gerry Mulligan, led by five musicians who had performed with the great baritone saxophonist. The concert concluded at 6:00 p.m. Figuring the musicians would need time to pack up, we took our time to wander over to the nearby restaurant, arriving at six thirty. The band arrived a few minutes before eight. Nobody was in a hurry.

Appetizers were ordered, a round of beverages arrived, and dinner orders were taken. Around the table, the main course was the conversation. A notable trumpeter had damaged his lip. A favorite nightclub was closing its doors. Funny stories were told. The group's pianist recounted a riotous story about a saxophonist who kept creating even when he was on an oxygen tank. News was shared. The horn player next to me shared that a mutual acquaintance had been denied a significant grant.

More appetizers appeared as another round of drinks arrived. Our party grew to fourteen while the restaurant patrons thinned out. Infectious bursts of laughter erupted at both ends of the table. More stories were told. Somebody told a joke. Then a web of compliments was spun by musicians and fans.

"Great concert today!"

"Loved that third tune in the second set."

"Man, you played your tail off."

"Wish Mulligan could have heard us."

"Glad he didn't!"

More laughter.

The long table didn't quiet down. The energy kept building long past the desserts and nightcaps were brought to the table.

When we departed sometime after 10:00 p.m. to begin an hour-long drive home, I looked at my very patient wife and said, "Welcome to the hang."

"HE BLESSED US"

A few years ago, the Jazz at Lincoln Center Orchestra performed a concert in Fayetteville, Arkansas. Led by trumpeter Wynton Marsalis, the sixteen-piece big band plays the best of the jazz repertoire. The band features some of the finest musicians in the world. The concert went well, but the band members were more excited about what was coming the next day.

It was an open date on their touring calendar, and they were going to visit the renowned trumpeter Clark Terry, the first African American to be hired by NBC Studios to join the Tonight Show Band. A monumental figure in the jazz pantheon, Terry had toured with Count Basie, Duke Ellington, and Quincy Jones. Now he had retired and was living in Arkansas, where he was struggling with a series of health challenges.

One of the band members said, "That open date is close to his ninety-fourth birthday. We won't be far from his house. Could we go and see him?"

It didn't take much to convince Marsalis. As Wynton said of Clark's influence on his own decision to play the trumpet, "His spectacular playing made me want to practice, but his warmth and optimism made me want to be a part of the world of jazz."

A few days before this side trip, they discovered Terry had been hospitalized with complications from diabetes. He was struggling. The Lincoln Center band members didn't miss a beat, declaring, "We can go to his house, or we can go to the hospital. It doesn't matter, but we are going to see Clark Terry." With little lead time, the hospital staff set up a special room where the band could wait for him to be brought in. The musicians arrived in two buses and an instrument truck. They set up quickly. Someone brought a birthday cake. As Clark was wheeled into the room in his hospital bed, the band began an informal concert.

After performing a handful of tunes, the band members went to Terry's bedside one at a time, leaned down, and introduced themselves into his hearing-assistance device. Clark greeted each one, shook their hands, and offered a positive word. The band reassembled to play a New Orleans version of "Happy Birthday." Clark blew out the candles on the cake, and there wasn't a dry eye in the place.

Marsalis reflected on that moving celebration, noting how generous Clark Terry had been with his life and music. Terry's work had influenced every member of the band through his concerts, recordings, musical instruction, and—most of all—his friendship. Noting how Clark's positive spirit had the power to lift up others, even as he was lying in a hospital bed near the end of his life, Wynton named it as a blessing.

The best blessings are reciprocal, and they are a part of what it means to be in a dynamic community. They don't merely trickle down from strong to weak; they are shared side by side. This is the nature of human community.

A jazz band takes a "free day" to go eight hours out of its way to bless their hero. He blesses them in return. There is generosity. There is love. There is a deep sense that each person was participating in the same life. This most holy life.

IMPROVISATION: HOW MANY MUSICIANS ARE IN YOUR QUARTET?

Every quartet needs a comedian.
We have five.

One dances naked by firelight.
We expect his heavy feet
to lift from the soil.

The second wisecracker
gives the monologue
that starts the laughter.

The third collects a sack of bland straw
and spins the whole lot into
threads of gold.

A fourth smirks on his bench,
convening the tornado
that swirls around him.

Who is the fifth joker,
serving up mirth?
The One who gives
all things birth.

CHAPTER TWELVE

PAYING BACK THE UNIVERSE
Swinging with Purpose

I'll always be dedicating my life to new causes and try to make this planet a better place and pay back wherever this universe comes from for being so good to me.

—bassist Charlie Haden

Don't ask what the world needs. Ask what makes you come alive and go do that. Because what the world needs is people who have come alive.

—mystic Howard Thurman

SOMEWHERE A LIGHT GOES ON

When Sherrie was a sixth-grade musician in the elementary-school band, her career began. The catalyst was a music teacher telling her, "The trumpet is not an instrument that girls play."

Sherrie took up the clarinet, followed by the cello. Neither choice took. When the same music teacher said, "I'm looking for a volunteer to play the bass drum," Sherrie raised her hand in frustration and asked, "I get to hit something?" She was in. It was an easy gig, full of quarter notes.

One day, the teacher announced that Buddy Rich, the famous drummer, was playing nearby with his Killer Force big band. On the night of the show, Sherrie sat in the auditorium as the lights went down. The band came out, and the crowd applauded as Buddy emerged from backstage and sat behind the drum set. Setting a pace on his cymbal, he counted off the first tune—"One, two, three, four"—and the band exploded into action.

One of the saxophonists stood to improvise a solo, and the crowd applauded again. But not Sherrie. She was so mesmerized by the drummer that her eyes remained trained on every beat he created. She had never heard anybody play like Buddy Rich. "I want to do that," Sherrie said to herself, watching him.

Sherrie Maricle couldn't know what the moment would signify. She had no idea that she would eventually earn three college degrees in music, including a PhD in percussion. She could not comprehend yet that in a few years, she would be performing regularly with bass legend Slam Stewart. Or that she would play percussion with the New York Pops in Carnegie Hall. Or that five years after Buddy Rich's death in 1987, she would be asked by the drummer's former manager to form an all-female big band of her own. With Sherrie on percussion, Diva was formed, an act with the tagline "No Man's Band." Nor could she have known that in 2009, the Kennedy Center would honor her with a Lifetime Achievement Award.

She didn't know any of that yet. All she knew was that she was going to be a drummer.

That's what happens when the light goes on. When Juan was a teenager tapping his foot. When Sherrie was transfixed by a drummer who changed her life's course. That's also what tapped the shoulder of Bobby McFerrin.

Although he's better known as a vocalist today, McFerrin began his music career as a piano player. He grew up with music in his family. His mother was a singer. His father was a star at the Metropolitan Opera and sang for the Hollywood film *Porgy and Bess*. But for Bobby, success was elusive. He scuffled for work and landed in

Salt Lake City, twenty-seven years old, newly married, and playing the piano to accompany dance students at University of Utah.

One day in January, he was walking home for a lunch break when he heard a voice. *The* Voice. "You are a singer now," The Voice said.

"I suddenly knew it in my bones," Bobby McFerrin said years later. He did not expect this. Neither did he dream of selling out concert venues around the world, recording a number one hit, or winning ten Grammy awards. But sometime between 12:00 and 12:30 p.m. on a January sidewalk in Salt Lake City, a Light illumined his soul, and he knew what he would do with his life. "A burning bush moment," he called it.

Thousands of years earlier, Moses was tending the flocks of his father-in-law, unaware that he would soon be the leader of a nation, no sense of what the future would hold when his name was called. His very own name. He stepped close to a bush that seemed to be on fire, and The Voice spoke to him, right where he was. And he stepped into the moment that would change everything.

At first glance, Moses was an unlikely candidate for the job. But in reality, God had uniquely equipped him for this very purpose. He brought everything he knew to the calling. His understanding of Pharaoh and Egyptian politics and systems, having been raised as an adopted son of the royal family. His ability to direct a flock of sheep, skills he later needed to lead wayward, distracted Hebrew slaves out of Egypt and into freedom. His firsthand experience with the burning bush seared his soul with the authenticity to bring everything to service of The Voice, the call.

In each of these cases, the past is the prologue. Moses became a leader unlike any other in history. Sherrie Maricle was already beating the drum but began to play in new, inspired ways. Bobby McFerrin brought his ability for accompanying other singers on the piano to understanding how voices could blend and overlap.

If we excavate these moments, we discover more beneath the surface. McFerrin, for instance, often claimed his greatest inspiration was his father. "He had such gratitude for his gift and was very humble," Bobby remembers. When his own moment of clarity came, it resonated as complete truth.

A brilliant quote comes to mind, one that some attribute to Mark Twain, though Twain scholars have never been able to substantiate this. It goes, "The two most important days in your life are the day you were born and the day you find out why." Perhaps the aphorism is too cheerful to have come from the old cynic, yet it points to the source of callings—that purpose, that why. Or, to turn this sentiment into a question, we might turn to Duke Ellington's song that nails it: "What Am I Here For?"

"BUT I DON'T HAVE A CALLING"

A sense of purpose can be elusive, especially if we take a job to pay the bills, to get by, to support the music. I have known great musicians who delivered flowers or medical prescriptions, drove cabs, and painted signs. Few of them have heroic stories to compare with the likes of Maricle, McFerrin, or Moses. Those stories seem special. Many of us have not had such flashy experiences, nor will we occupy such notable positions in history.

Perhaps you haven't heard The Voice. And if the truth is told, sometimes a well-polished story has been amplified by a sense of celebrity. Yet beneath the surface of each calling are clues for us.

Note that each of the people I've mentioned had an awakening that came in the middle of a mundane activity. They had an awareness that the strands of their life experience could be woven together. There was something intriguing about the revelatory moment that beckoned them forward. Each felt empowered by what they now knew, even if they did not know yet what it would demand of them. And if these were holy invitations, they were timely, arriving when the message from Headquarters was ready to be received.

In the life of a pastor, people drop by all the time to chat. Sometimes the conversations ramble. Other times they focus on specific questions or tasks. Beneath the talking, I, in my day job, often wonder what other Mystery might be lurking. In a pregnant pause, I might even find the courage to ask, "Why are you here?" This is always awkward. Maybe the visitor was simply looking for a good cup of coffee. Or a friendly connection with someone who would take them seriously. Perhaps something else is perking in their soul. Often it is not the right time to plumb the depths and clarify their reason for existence. I get that. It takes a while for meaning to bubble up. But sometimes asking the question changes things.

Not all jazz musicians have the words to describe it, but they have discovered they are on the planet to make music. Most will be neither rich nor famous nor have the story of their calling recorded in print. But each one can answer the question "Why are you here?" They're musicians because they *must* be musicians.

Most of the true music-makers, the truthful praise-makers, know the secret strength of their art. Ask a jazz musician "Why do you work for near-poverty wages, in abysmal conditions, in uncertain times, for people who do not value your God-given gifts?" and many will respond with the kind of clarity that comes with a calling. "The music," they say, "is more important than me."

Music brings them alive. That's why they welcome jazz, shape it, and invent it. They have discovered that is why they are here. This is the experience of a calling. And it is not unique to musicians.

There are teachers who feel this way, plumbers who believe they are called to their vocation, social workers who have found life's purpose in their work, and plenty of retired people who are finally doing what they have always been on fire to do.

When I was fifteen, the activity director of a nearby nursing home asked me to come and play half an hour of piano music for the residents. It was my first gig. I had never been to a nursing home, but how difficult could it be? At the time, I was immersing myself in ragtime, so I bundled up my Scott Joplin books, asked my mother to give me a ride, and went to make some music.

I was not prepared for my own fragility or the fragile lives of those I played for that day. There were people in wheelchairs who could not speak. An old man with crippled hands tried in vain to clap. A lady moaned whenever she enjoyed a song, sometimes when I was already into the next one. There were funky smells in the air. A disembodied voice on an intercom regularly interrupted the performance.

At the end of the short concert, I went out to the station wagon and wept. I—and my music—had entered a world entirely unknown to me.

To my surprise, I received a thank-you note from the activity director, reporting the residents were thrilled by my music. I did not realize it at the time, but somewhere between my shock and their joy was the first tug to do my life's work.

Why am I here? To pray the piano.

I make music, care for people, spend time with those in need, and do a lot of other things, necessary and otherwise. These days, I enjoy visiting the local nursing home to bang out some syncopated hymns and serve communion to people who are hungry for joy and good news. It may be the most important thing that I do all month. It's not the only thing I do, but it lies so close to what God wants to get done.

It isn't the only thing that God wants to get done, but it is one thing to be done that I can do. And because it's jazz, what blesses outward blesses inward and everywhere else.

WHAT THE ILLUMINATION REQUIRES

A couple of years after my experience in the nursing home, I was selected to play the piano for a statewide high school jazz ensemble. Phil Woods was the guest soloist, and the saxophonist brought his Grammy-award-winning quartet to perform for the second half of the evening concert. We rehearsed in the morning, and after lunch, Phil led a clinic for the student musicians.

One of the hotshots in the band stepped up to play a tune by Charlie Parker. Woods cut him off almost immediately. "What are you doing?" he barked, deflating the student's tires. "You haven't learned the tune correctly. Your intonation is sharp. You're picking some terrible notes for your solo."

All of us who observed made the instant decision that we would not step onto that stage. Phil was fierce.

After he settled down from that tantrum, Woods offered some foundational advice: "Learn your instrument." He did not elaborate. Did he mean jazz? Classical? Musical scales? Instrumental studies or masterworks? It didn't matter. He implored that gathering of teenagers to develop the highest musical skills. "You want to get to the point," he said, "where you can play whatever a conductor puts on your music stand, free enough to play whatever you hear in your imagination."

That doesn't happen without a lot of work, but a teacher can keep us on task and unlock issues we did not know existed.

For a short time in high school, I took weekly piano lessons from a local musical legend named Lenny. He had traveled the country in the big-band era and settled down to marry a secretary in the office of our high school. I used to cling to his insights, in large part because I paid him twenty dollars for a thirty-minute lesson, a sum equivalent to my income from mowing four lawns.

Lenny taught me a great deal about the harmonies and rhythms of jazz. But most of all, he said that when it comes to art, one can only learn so much from the printed page. One afternoon, he listened to me play. After sucking the life out of a Kool Menthol, he said, "You know, I can teach you how to swing melodies and lay down hip chords, but that won't make you a musician. If you want to play jazz, you must study what you hear and then play it."

Lenny's assignment was to listen to recordings, capture the notes in the air, and write them down on paper. It was hard work. But there are no shortcuts for understanding how music moves, for following where the calling leads.

STANDING ON ANOTHER'S SHOULDERS

"The first step of artistic growth is imitation," says David Liebman, deemed a Jazz Master by the National Endowment of the Arts.

Jazz is art, not merely craft. It is music-making far more than technique. There are dialects to mimic, phrases to spin, models to emulate. Just as young children learn speech from adults, the growing artist learns syntax as well as vocabulary from the masters. We immerse ourselves in order to absorb. As one trumpeter told me, "This is Miles Davis month for me. Last month was Roy Eldridge; next month is Dizzy Gillespie."

Long before I met David, I found an early book he wrote to describe the process of working with a jazz group. It is full of mysteries explained: how an improvised solo can rise and fall like the plot of a short story, how harmonies may intensify as a song develops, how a saxophonist interacts with a drummer, and how the whole enterprise depends on attentive listening by everyone in the group. The book was helpful, but it was watching Liebman blow his soprano sax with his quartet that was a master class bringing the pages to life.

Earlier, I recounted the story of Miles Davis firing John Coltrane in the spring of 1957, prompting the spiritual awakening that began in the saxophonist. Coltrane tells us of a musical awakening that was going on in the course of events. When Thelonious Monk, the quirky bop pianist, hired him immediately afterward, Coltrane found Monk's music challenging, like "stepping into an empty elevator shaft."

"Working with Thelonious Monk brought me close to a musical architect of the highest order," he later wrote. "I felt I learned from him in every way—through the senses, theoretically, technically. I would talk to Monk about musical problems, and he would sit at the piano and show me the answers by playing them. I could watch him play and find out the things I wanted to know. Also, I could see a lot of things that I didn't know about at all."

The calling cannot be fully claimed without the help of others. As jazz great Wayne Shorter is said to have once quipped, the short person who stands on the shoulders of the giant will be able to see further than the giant.

ON EMPTYING ONESELF

One day, I received a phone call at my church office. The caller was exuberant, chattering a mile a minute without saying who he was. When he took a breath, he introduced himself as Kent Groff, a fellow Presbyterian minister, who had read an article on jazz that I had written for a seminary publication. He and I had graduated from the same school almost twenty years apart.

We set a date to meet for dinner. Just as soon as we ordered our food, he jumped in. "You talk about losing yourself when you play jazz," he said. "Is that like kenosis?"

I knew the word from my New Testament Greek studies. *Kenosis* is the word used to describe the movement of Jesus from heaven to earth. "He emptied himself," Paul writes in his letter to the Philippian church, "taking the form of a slave, being born in human likeness." It was an act of complete humility, total immersion, with no regard for reward or success.

"*Kenosis*," Kent said again. "Is that what jazz is like?"

I liked Kent instantly and appreciated the ways he understood the profound relationship between spiritual formation and jazz. "That, Kent," I said, "is exactly what jazz is like."

As I soon discovered, Dr. Groff has a calling to ask big questions. As a spiritual director, he has offered a listening ear and companionship to fellow pilgrims who wished to deepen their spiritual life. He also plays a bit of jazz piano. In one of his fine books, *Active Spirituality: A Guide for Seekers and Ministers*, he captures something in words I have long sought to articulate: "The Christ-life is the pattern for understanding and redeeming all of life's experiences. Some emptying needs to happen before we can be filled. *Kenosis* is the model for genuine spiritual 'formation,' the creative transformation of suffering."

Whether soul-making or jazz-making, the essential work is formation. Both speak to the why, and both empty themselves for a different kind of filling. Jazz emerges from suffering but will not

THRIVING ON A RIFF

be contained by it. It is death and resurrection, not in a three-day weekend but in a singular moment. It is Louis Armstrong lifting the spirits of people in a town in western Pennsylvania, where he would not fit in during daylight. It is Dave Brubeck refusing to let skin color determine who will play in his band or to compromise his values for the sake of financial success. It is Mary Lou Williams offering syncopation to heal broken hearts and twisted spirits. It is Jimmy Greene announcing musically that love wins, no matter what.

Musicians cannot become deep souls without emptying themselves, without losing themselves in music that lives by the virtues of honesty, vitality, and freedom. As they surrender their will to the creative process, they lay their souls open to be shaped by grace. It is analogous to any other repeated activity in life. The more you practice it, the more it shapes you.

In his obituary in the *New York Times*, the luminous bassist Gary Peacock was quoted to offer a final lesson for us all:

> The question is, How much are you willing to give up to play this music? I don't think it can work if you still have an agenda, if you feel you still need to prove something musically. That's not the point. It's just about the music. So you're going to serve that, not yourself or somebody in the audience, not the critics or the reviewers. It's just the music.

To relieve human suffering. To empty ourselves so music can transform us. To help someone learn to trust again. To put food in somebody else's stomach. To mend the broken-hearted. To set somebody free. To put a song in the air. There are burning bushes all along our paths and no shortage of invitations and callings given to each one of us.

One thing is clear to me: to take your life's calling seriously is to stand on holy ground. To stand empty before that ground so that something greater can happen. It is the place where God meets you, where God invites you to make a difference, where God promises that kenosis is the key to freedom.

IMPROVISATION: SOMEBODY'S CALLING

Maybe you believed you were on your own,
self-made,
your only purpose to follow your nose
and consume your appetites.
Yet in the earthquake, the Voice speaks,
a sidewalk is shattered,
and you walk the awkward path
ever forward.

Maybe you assumed you could put in your time,
slide down to Boca
and play shuffleboard till they sank you.
Then your independence is interrupted,
and you learn like an infant
how you were never your own.
You belong to the patch of soil where
you are planted. Glorify it while there is time,
for you will fertilize it soon enough.

Maybe you hoped they would leave you
alone, no one would notice your absence,
much less your presence.

But anonymity is not an option.
Not to One who loves you before you were
a twinkle in Daddy's eye and a dot
in Mama's womb.
To be known is to be called for,
enlivened, and sent.

The Voice reveals designs for you;
consider what they are.
Advance to the intersection of
your bliss and
the broken world's need.

For some of us,
we hear the Voice say,
"Let there be music."
Who are we
to refuse?

CHAPTER THIRTEEN

JAZZ IN THE CATHEDRAL AND OTHER GREAT IDEAS

There is nothing irreligious in rhythm, nothing particularly ethnic. It's a gift from God, like everything else.

—*Father Norman O'Connor*

AN IDEA IN A BATHTUB

It was a mess. Chuck Gompertz slumped in the bathwater. A young Episcopalian priest, he had committed the unforgivable career mistake. One morning in 1964, he had phoned the bishop to criticize him for something he'd seen in the newspaper.

Bishop James Pike had offered recent updates on the completion of Grace Cathedral in San Francisco. This was a significant matter for the city, and the bishop announced it would be celebrated with a "Year of Grace." Part of that celebratory year, the news article announced, would be a "holy hootenanny" with the teens.

Rev. Gompertz, all of twenty-eight years old, full of himself and feeling righteous, was offended. Without thinking through the ramifications, he dialed the bishop's office and was stunned when Pike answered his own phone.

"Bishop," he said, "I must take offense at something I saw in the newspaper. For something as significant as the completion of a great cathedral, I don't think we should be talking about a holy hootenanny."

Pike listened as the young priest declared his dismay. Then Pike said, "Okay, now it's your job. Fill the cathedral in May 1965." Handing over the responsibility, the bishop hung up the phone.

I'm finished, Chuck thought. He imagined the worst. After criticizing the bishop, he could expect to be sent to a string of struggling parishes for the rest of his career. He did the only reasonable thing. He drew a warm bath.

As he recounted the moment to me fifty years later, the two of us sitting together in his living room, Chuck remembered simmering in the bathwater. Had he done the right thing? Should he have stood up for his principles? Why did he keep putting his foot in his mouth? How would he ever fill up an enormous cathedral? What in the world would he do?

As his mind raced and his body began to slightly relax, a song suddenly floated in from the next room. The local radio station was playing a lively jazz tune that had been getting a lot of airplay in recent months. It was fresh, melodic, and had a lilt to it. The announcer called the song "Cast Your Fate to the Wind," and Chuck thought, *That's what I have just done.* Suddenly an idea sparked in his imagination. What if he could fill the cathedral with a jazz mass?

He climbed out of the tub, pulled on a robe, and called the radio station. How could he get in touch with the musician who wrote and recorded that song? The station manager gave him the number of Fantasy Records, a local company. He called Fantasy Records and spoke to somebody there. That's how he got the phone number of a Bay Area pianist by the name of Vince Guaraldi.

Gompertz dialed the number, and Guaraldi's wife answered. The priest offered his idea to her, a concept that was still evolving. She said, "Let me get him." After a few minutes, Guaraldi got on the phone. He listened to the pitch, then said, "Bach, Brahms, and Beethoven all wrote masses, so why not me?" They planned to meet for lunch a week later, which gave Chuck some time to refine his idea.

Many months later, Grace Cathedral was filled for the premiere of Vince Guaraldi's mass on May 21, 1965. It was the first jazz mass presented as a worship service in an American cathedral.

By all accounts, it was a holy hootenanny.

NOT A NEW IDEA

Rev. Chuck Gompertz didn't know it at the time, but he wasn't the first to cook up the idea of welcoming jazz into a congregation's worship service. That honor likely belongs to Frank Tirro, former dean of the Yale School of Music. While a student at University of Nebraska, he received a commission to compose a jazz mass. A talented clarinetist, saxophonist, composer, and church choir director, his "American Jazz Mass" appeared in 1959. It was presented widely in the United States, Canada, and Europe.

Ed Summerlin, a saxophonist and jazz educator, was also an early pioneer in jazz worship services. During his last semester of college, his nine-month-old daughter died from a congenital heart defect. The crisis devastated him. A concerned professor connected him with a local pastor. Summerlin did not have much connection to the church, but the pastor encouraged him to translate his grief into music. He composed "Requiem for Mary Jo" (1959) and developed a jazz setting of the United Methodist daily prayer service, which he recorded as *Liturgical Jazz*. His music received great reviews from jazz magazines and mixed reviews from the public. He would later serve as the musical director for *Look Up and Live*, an inspiring religious broadcast on the CBS network, which occasionally featured jazz musicians such as trumpeter Freddie Hubbard and bassist Ron Carter.

Lalo Schifrin may be a more familiar name to many of us. Born to a Jewish family in Buenos Aires, Schifrin composed *Jazz Suite on the Mass Texts* the year before Guaraldi's mass. Recorded in 1964 by the flutist Paul Horn, it was a daring work that would not find its way into a worship service for many years. It grew in popularity after Schifrin became well known, first as the pianist in one of Dizzy Gillespie's groups and later as the composer of numerous scores for film and television, including the theme of the television show *Mission Impossible*.

The creative ferment was at work. No doubt, it originated in the church's attempt to reach a new generation through the 1960s, blending equal parts of experimentation and novelty. From the perspective of jazz musicians, it became a way to express religious faith, particularly in the context of the growing civil rights movement.

Led by pianist Mary Lou Williams, many skilled musicians began to create jazz for the church. Williams's first religious composition, "St. Martin de Porres" (1962), honored the first saint from the Western Hemisphere to be canonized by the Roman church. Over the next decade, she would compose an impressive amount of religious music, including three different jazz masses.

Like Ed Summerlin, Dave Brubeck was led by grief to set words from the Bible to music after his nephew Philip died of a brain tumor in 1966. To work through his feelings, he created a jazz setting of the words of Jesus, "Let not your heart be troubled; ye believe in God, believe also in me." He offered this choral piece to his family as a gift of consolation. With their encouragement, he continued to draft more jazz and choral settings of the words of Christ, which debuted as the major oratorio *The Light in the Wilderness* (1968). By the end of his life, Brubeck had written a dozen more sacred oratorios, several choral anthems, and a mass.

Eddie Bonnemere was also a key figure in the development of sacred jazz. Raised in a Roman Catholic school, he taught in the New York City public school system, directed church choirs, and performed with his jazz quartet. In May 1966, he premiered his *Missa Hodierna* at New York's St. Charles Borromeo Catholic Church with a thirteen-piece jazz group and mixed choir. It was reportedly the first time that jazz would be included in the Roman Catholic liturgy. Bonnemere went on to compose at least five more jazz masses—four for the Catholics and one for the Lutherans. He was also a frequent collaborator with Rev. John Garcia Gensel in creating music for the weekly jazz vespers at St. Peter's Lutheran Church.

Noting the popularity of Guaraldi's work, the leadership of Grace Cathedral invited Duke Ellington in on the act, securing Ellington's band for a concert during the "Year of Grace" while Guaraldi's mass still was being developed. When they approached Ellington—with far more enthusiasm than they had shown to Guaraldi—Duke shrugged off any notion that it would be a jazz mass or worship service. "These concerts are not the traditional mass jazzed up," he said. "I think of myself as a messenger boy, one who tries to bring messages to those who were more or less raised with the guidance of the Church."

Rather than a mass or jazz liturgy, Ellington created a "concert of sacred music," presented at Grace Cathedral for the first time on September 16, 1965. It was a huge success and would establish the trajectory for the remainder of his performing career. Ellington repeated this sacred concert in many venues around the world, later creating two more sacred concert programs that were also repeated many times. When he reflected on this new dimension in his work, Duke often said, "It's the most important thing I've ever done."

APPLAUSE IS NEVER UNANIMOUS

The affirmation that Ellington received, however, was not universal. In his extraordinary study *Lift Every Voice and Swing*, scholar Vaughn Booker reports that the greatest resistance to Duke's sacred concerts came from the Black church. In fact, one large association of urban Baptist pastors overwhelmingly passed a resolution "against endorsing the Ellington performance." There was grave concern that Duke, a well-known womanizer, did not possess the requisite moral qualities to bring his music into the church. One preacher went so far as to declare, "We think the man himself is incapable of writing sacred music."

There were other concerns that the music might "get out of hand," especially in those congregations that rejected the emotionalism of revivals and had worked hard to climb the ladder of social respectability. This is a recurring theme in the churches I've known. One elderly woman struggled with the experience of the new form as she sat through one of the first jazz worship services that I led for my congregation. Afterward, when she finally found the words, she said, "Rev. Carter, that music was so wonderful that I almost tapped my feet." Almost!

In my conversation with Chuck Gompertz, he vividly recalled the resistance he faced in bringing Vince Guaraldi to Grace Cathedral. The mass was featured in a full-page article in *Time Magazine*, and in response, Gompertz received hate mail from people he had never met. "You've hit the big time," his mother remarked after she read about the mass in *Readers Digest*, not realizing her son was receiving anonymous threats. One ominous warning came in a plain white envelope on a single sheet of paper. The writer reported that he knew the movements of Chuck's first-grade daughter, where she went to school, and what time she was walking down the street. "We don't like what you're doing to the Church," it read, "and to music in the Church. We are watching you."

Resistance also was revealed in passive-aggressive behavior. Gompertz affirms that the bishop and his diocesan staff were deeply supportive of the event. As for the cathedral staff, however, "they were petty and difficult to work with; they kept throwing obstacles up."

"Pure pettiness and competition," Chuck noted, "but we pulled it off in spite of it all."

WHAT EXPERIENCE REVEALS

Personally, after thirty years of welcoming jazz into Christian worship services, I have seen it all. Some worshippers leave bursting with joy, others are burdened with frowns, and a few offer expressions of utter confusion. Rarely, though, has anybody been bored. All have discovered that jazz offers more than fresh music to take in; there are also dancing saxophonists and singing drummers to experience. As for the musicians I've invited, most have enthusiastically agreed to play, although a few have turned me down.

The sweet spot for jazz worship can be found when both sides of the equation are respected, with neither diminished. I admit, it isn't always smooth sailing. Once, a bassist pulled out a cigarette when the service concluded. Unable to find his pack of matches, he began to lean toward a lit altar candle before I asked him to please light up outside.

In addition to providing music in our house of worship, the Presbybop Quartet also performs on the road, and I recall one church our band visited where there was a frosty moment as the pastor insisted on a cold formality. She demanded that she pray with the musicians before the service, turning her prayer into a diatribe about order and propriety. As soon as she said, "Amen," the saxophonist looked up at me and said, "She doesn't really want us here, does she!"

And then there was the jazz vespers service led by a piano trio with no sense that it was a gathering for prayer and spiritual formation. They played a medley of Cole Porter tunes; made no attempt to connect with the church, the spirit of the event, or the hymns of that community; and yawned when the preacher tried to salvage the moment with a few heartfelt thoughts.

To me, that is what was so remarkable about the Vince Guaraldi Mass. Since the experience was new, the jazz group accompanied hymns that the congregation already knew. The melodies were mostly in quarter notes at a singable tempo. Jazz happened in the fresh harmonies and the improvisations around the edges. Rev. Gompertz also selected a favorite mass setting, the *Missa Marialis*, which Episcopalians of that era knew well. Guaraldi's trio provided a bossa nova foundation as the choir chanted over the top. And Barry Mineah, the choir director for the event, took a deep breath when he realized the band never rehearsed the music the same way twice.

The outcome of a jazz worship service can be rehearsed, but it will resist being managed. As one of my musical colleagues once quipped after dealing with a choir director with control issues, "If they didn't want jazz musicians to play, why did they invite us?" It was a fair question.

PREPPING FOR THE CATHEDRAL

In September 1992, I created my first jazz worship service for my congregation, and it happened practically by accident. Our church's organist planned a vacation around Labor Day and could not find a substitute for the Sunday service. In a moment of desperation, she asked me at a committee meeting if I could play the hymns. I was glad to accept.

With a twinkle in her eye, she added, "Will you be jazzing up the hymns?"

Since that September, we have built a jazz ministry alongside an excellent church music program. In any given year, the church plans three dedicated jazz services, including a Labor Day celebration that frequently focuses on the music of a notable musician, a late-night Christmas Eve communion service, and a Mardi Gras gala with hats, horns, colored beads, and feather boas. The church regularly invites jazz groups to play for its annual concert series. Sometimes it is the professional ensemble I formed, the Presbybop Quartet (short for "Presbyterian Bebop"), after our first jazz service.

The Presbybop band, in various configurations, has created several recordings and performed countless times around the country, expanding the ministry. As a quartet, we specialize in creating joy and building a sense of community.

In addition to the challenges of juggling both halves of my brain, I've had the occasional challenge of finding fresh musical material. That was the case on Christmas Day, 2014, after a two-hour jazz service that concluded in the wee hours of the morning. We had done it all. What could we do next?

When I realized that 2015 would be the fiftieth anniversary of the most popular jazz soundtrack in the country, *A Charlie Brown Christmas*, we began to shape the next Christmas Eve jazz service around that music, especially since the band already played a lot of those classic compositions written by none other than Vince Guaraldi. And when I recalled that he presented the mass at Grace Cathedral in 1965, a second fiftieth anniversary was planned. Our Labor Day service would be the perfect time to offer it.

But as I considered the mass, I wondered where to begin. Emails to Grace Cathedral quickly revealed that written scores to the Guaraldi Mass did not exist. Vince never wrote anything down. The choir had sung directly from the red Episcopal hymnal, which had gone out of print, replaced by newer versions. The collaboration was well-rehearsed, but it still happened on the fly—in the presence of two thousand souls.

I decided to start transcribing the recording, putting the essential notes and harmonies from 1965 on paper. It was a monumental task, but Derrick Bang, Guaraldi's brilliant biographer, helped and became a good friend in the process. He offered much of the storied background that informs this chapter. I also reached out to my friend Jim Martinez, a jazz pianist in California and a serious Guaraldi aficionado. Martinez took the idea and ran with it. As I sent him copies of my transcriptions, he cooked up his own idea. What if, in addition to the mass at my church, we held a fiftieth-anniversary celebration in Grace Cathedral, the location of the original Guaraldi Mass? He then booked "the big room" where it all began. Jim asked me to take part, and on August 15, 2015, we had a holy hootenanny of our own. I preached the sermon. Jim's trio and choir brought to life the music that had not been heard in five decades.

In attendance was Rev. Chuck Gompertz, sitting in the front row, nearing the end of his career. On hearing the mass again in its new iteration, he wept tears of joy.

SOMETIMES A FAMILY REUNION

Sometimes the church forgets its roots and remains indifferent to jazz, yet it is inevitable that jazz and the church reunite. They both emerge from experiences of suffering. They breathe the same air. They inhale the same Spirit. They provide a shared witness to the same vitality. They reveal the depths and heights of what it means to be human. They teach us that the spiritual life is *this* life, not merely the next life, and they infuse life with a rhythm, harmony, and creativity beyond all measured expectations.

For me, worship is where the intersection is given completeness. Worship is where all who are in the room are invited to lose themselves in wonder, love, and praise. Jazz can amplify the moment and welcome the Holy as a life-giving event.

When our church held the anniversary celebration of the Guaraldi Mass, these are the words I preached that reflected not only on the present moment but that intersection of spirit, worship, and jazz, that holy meeting experience:

> What I have learned about jazz in the church is that people really want it. Even if they sit scowling with their arms crossed, they really want it. They want to be in the presence of the energy and imagination. They want the passion to kiss them alive. They want their own frozen hearts to defrost. And it's not the jazz per se; it is what's behind the jazz. They want to know there is a deep joy at the center of the universe that has the power to make all things well.

Deep joy. All things well. And always, where jazz comes in, the *yes . . . and.*

IMPROVISATION: HOMILY FROM THE FIFTIETH ANNIVERSARY OF THE GUARALDI MASS

It is good to be in the house
where jazz was officially welcomed into worship.
This is the place . . .
but if truth be told,
jazz was in the church long before that.

Jazz crept in through the side door.
When forced laborers arrived from Africa,
they brought the five-note scales they knew so well.
As those notes bumped into the tempered notes
of their European importers and overseers,
the clashing notes turned blue.
God was in the blues.
That is how jazz feels.

Jazz sneaked into the pulpit long before.
Any time a preacher reads three or four verses of scripture
and then talks for eighteen more minutes,
you hear all of the new material that bubbled up

from the jambalaya of study, prayer, reflection,
perspiration and holy inspiration,
all the while simmering in the pot of human need.
The dots on the page created a conversation in the air.
That is how jazz sounds.

Jazz has stood in the narthex,
as ushers had to improvise
where they would seat the unexpected strangers.
Jazz has robed itself in the sacristy,
when the servers ask,
"Do we have enough bread to feed all these people?"
Jazz has been abiding in the church from the beginning,
because wherever the Holy Spirit is, Jazz is.

And this is the house where Jazz was first welcomed.
By all accounts, it was a bumpy welcome.
Critics had dismissed jazz as saloon music,
forgetting that the whole earth is the Lord's,
and any ground can become holy ground,
God willing.

Buffoons dismissed jazz out of their racist dispositions,
believing it unworthy of a God who creates everybody.

And the Pharisees are still out there,
declaring Jazz is not worthy of their spiritual superiority.
If it touches them, they could get infected.
They might even tap their feet to God's drummer.

But wherever the Holy Spirit is, Jazz is.

That is why people can get offended.
They don't want God to get too close.
They are anxious about defrosting

and leaving puddles on the floor.
They worry the Spirit of God may blow wild and free,
and something might happen that is not written down
on the worship bulletin.

When Jazz was welcomed here,
the moment was marked by hymns sung
to the wild, unpredictable, life-giving Spirit of God.
Imagine that.
"Come Holy Ghost, our hearts inspire,
and lighten with celestial fire."

On that day, angular syncopations and clashes of
    dissonance
became the moment for the Spirit to dance
as the soul of Christ breathed fresh life.
That is the best reason to welcome Jazz into this or any
    church:
to keep the church from suffocating
on piety that has run out of breath.

We live in fearful times, you know. Almost as fearful as
    1965.
The fundamentalist still fears the Holy Spirit,
frightened that God might do something
that hasn't yet been written down.
Rather than embrace the hard work
of living the life of Christ here and now,
the fearful Pharisee still cherry-picks a few favorite verses
to wield as blunt objects,
living an unconverted, unloving life.

It is challenging for anyone to follow the Christ
who still touches the leper,
heals the hemorrhage,

and repeatedly crosses the boundary into Gentile land.
It is demanding for the Christian to follow the Christ
off the page and into the real world.
But as we hear the Mass of Guaraldi
with the ancient chants ignited by
the rhythms of Brazil and harmonies of California,
let us affirm that a life of health and holiness
must be lived out here and now.

Where Jazz is, the Holy Spirit is.

This is the Spirit of God who loves the world, the whole
    world,
the world that yearns to be whole.
God goes into the world through Jesus to replace fear
    with awe,
violence with reconciliation, love-for-self-alone with love
    for all.
God's love is just that expansive and life-giving.

And should that love be crucified, it will begin again.
This is eternal love,
resisted by many,
yet persistently inviting us to become a new creation
in the power of the Spirit.
The world cannot turn out the Light that God sends to it,
neither can the church quench the Spirit's fire
by splashing holy water on it,
for it is God's intent to bring us completely alive.

When the Spirit comes,
the ankle bone is connected to the leg bone,
the ten little toe bones start tapping,
and all God's children shall dance.
Isn't that what we want, more than anything else?

Thank God for this house where Jazz was officially
    welcomed,
for the saints who made it happen,
for the Spirit who fills us with the joy of Jesus.

Grace Cathedral, San Francisco
August 15, 2015

CHAPTER FOURTEEN

DOES THIS SONG EVER END?

Jazz is the sound of God laughing. And I believe in it.

—Colleen Shaddox

I believe in the ultimate victory of faith, hope, and love in a world full of conflict and destruction.

—Dave Brubeck

THE GIFT THAT DID NOT END

Wow! My wife had gotten me concert tickets for my birthday. We were going to hear Béla Fleck and the Flecktones, an imaginative quartet with an electric banjo player at the helm. They blur the lines of musical styles, mixing up a jambalaya of bluegrass, jazz, and world music. The tickets were for a midweek concert at a jazz festival, scheduled for 7:00 p.m., at a venue about two hours from home. We arranged for a full evening: leave work early, grab some dinner nearby, and drive back home after the show. The next day, we planned to get up and go to work as usual.

We didn't know the concert would be almost four hours long.

The seats were a tight fit in the middle of the row. The band came out and played for an hour. Then three of them left the stage while the bass player played a fifteen-minute solo. When he finished, the rest of the band came back on, and the whole group played for another forty-five minutes. Then the drummer began his solo as the other band members stepped offstage. Then the rest of the quartet came out . . . and we could guess how this was going to go.

I loved every minute of it and sat on the edge of my narrow seat. My wife loved the first hour, but that was about her threshold. She must have whispered five or six times, "When is this going to end?"

When creative musicians have fun onstage, they lose all track of time. And when people listen to a group of musicians caught up in their craft, well, I presume that's why the audience is there.

Jazz musicians caught up in their songs, as I see and experience it, participate in the language of heaven.

REACHING BEYOND THE STARS

In the fourth chapter of the book of Revelation, a door swings open, and one sound is heard: a trumpet. Or, rather, it is a heavenly voice that sounds like a trumpet. The prophet John is invited by the trumpet voice into the eternal realm.

John grasps for words in his attempt to describe the beauty he sees in the heavenly beings around the central throne. Yet John is crystal clear in the language he uses to record what he *hears*. The eternal realm is filled with music. Wherever the Holy is, heaven is full of song. The heavenly court offers an unceasing hymn of praise, "Holy, holy, holy!"

This scene is repeated many times in the drama of the Bible's concluding book. John declares the primary reality of the universe is doxology, the praise of God. The song is ecstatic. It is liberating. It is the final expression of justice. The song rises above everything we know down here. Joy runs through the blood vessels of heaven. Love wins.

Once in a while, we humans hear that song. In recent years, people of faith have rediscovered an old Gospel hymn composed by Baptist preacher Robert Lowry after the Civil War. Most of the church hymnals ignored it until the folksinger Pete Seeger popularized the tune in the 1960s, with the first verse declaring:

My life flows on in endless song;
Above earth's lamentation,
I hear the sweet, tho' far-off hymn
That hails a new creation;
Thro' all the tumult and the strife
I hear the music ringing;
It finds an echo in my soul—
How can I keep from singing?

This is the eternal tune of the spiritual life: that God has won over the rebellions of this and every age, that God has already healed the brokenness of human life, that God has already reconciled earth to heaven.

From the vantage of earth, it does not look that way. But when the door swings open in the sky, we overhear the choirs singing and see the saints swinging from the chandeliers. Religious experts call this *eschatology*, literally the word about the last things. I call it *the song that never ends*.

TAKE HOLD OF THE LIFE THAT REALLY IS LIFE

An authentic spiritual life holds this vision in tension with the world as we know it. We must never let go of heaven nor earth.

If there is racism, disease, war, or bitterness among us, we have our cue that these things will not last into God's eternity. Similarly, if we know where everything is headed, we never have to settle for the bad news that bombards us every day and night. The Holy and the future-eternal is about something else.

The yearning for transcendence—that's what jazz musicians reach for in the right note, the beautiful note, the holy note. It is a gift from somewhere far beyond us that meets us in the specificity of our own broken circumstances. Musicians strive for a lifetime to play the one note that really counts. Some of them hear what others cannot yet hear.

Back in the bebop era, Bud Powell was one of the greatest pianists of the 1940s and 1950s. He was a contemporary of saxophonist Charlie Parker, and he lived a similarly chaotic and troubled life. When he was a young man, he was arrested while wandering drunk through the streets of Philadelphia. The police beat him brutally while he was detained. Left incoherent by the experience, he was sent to a psychiatric institution. Friends reported that he was never the same after that experience. From then on, when he wasn't on a bandstand making astonishing piano improvisations, he was frequently in and out of psychiatric hospitals. Bud Powell was a great musician and a troubled human being.

One of Powell's contemporaries recounts an instance of visiting him in the hospital. Bud was characteristically intense, and his visitor noticed that he had taken a pen and drawn the outlines of piano keys on the white walls of his room. Suddenly Bud jumped up, put his fingers on the keys, and began to bang his hands against the wall. "Listen to that," he said. "What do you think of these chords?" In his imagination, beyond his confinement, maybe beyond his wellness, Bud Powell heard music.

Tragically, like so many jazz musicians, Bud Powell had a short life. Consumed by addiction, diagnosed with schizophrenia, he died at age forty-one. This was a troubled human being whose delusions got the better of him. At least, you could choose to hear the story that way. The other way to hear the story is to notice how it points to the truth: when we get right to the heart of all reality, we hear music.

The book of Revelation is the trumpet note that understands the story in this way. The final book of the Bible is full of visions that unsettle the stomach. It is an unfolding drama with all the intense images of a science-fiction novel. Yet it is a book full of songs. There are lyrics and tunes on every page. In fact, the book of Revelation is second only to the book of Psalms in providing words that work their way to the Christian hymnal.

According to the book of Revelation, there is a new song beyond the bruises and brutalities of this age. At times, it is nearly impossible to hear. When the world wears us down, we are tempted to so wallow in the pain that we neglect the music we were made to make. When the music intersects with the spiritual life, if it carries us toward the Holy, the song has the power to set us free.

This music reminds me of a piece of graffiti I once saw in New York:

> You can punch my lips so I can't blow my horn,
> but my fingers will find a piano.
> You can slam the piano lid on my fingers,
> but you can't stop my toes from tapping like a drum.
> You can stomp on my foot to keep my toes from tapping,
> but my heart will keep swinging in four-four time.
> You can even stop my heart from ticking,
> but the music of the saints shall never cease.

Is there truly a new song like this? Yes. Written on subway walls, written in the book of Revelation, both pointing to the one reality beyond everything we can see or touch. It is a song sung by those who know the eternal power of grace. All who sing it have endured the pain and suffering of the world, and pain and suffering will not have the last word over them.

This is the song that sustains us, the only song large enough to do: a doxology—a song that praises God.

WHAT A LITTLE MOON DANCE CAN DO

In the film *The Fabulous Baker Boys* (1989), there is a scene where Jack Baker, jazz pianist, slips away from his brother, Frank, who runs the piano duo act that takes them to lounges around Seattle. Jack has had enough of the commercial nonsense of the pop music scene. He disappears into a jazz club to play the music he wants to play.

In the film, the look on his face while playing music at the jazz club is extraordinary: joy, ecstasy, brilliance, vulnerability, and delight, all at once. He loves what he is doing. For the moment, it doesn't matter if he gets paid. When a colleague spots him, she reads his face instantly. She knows he is doing more than dusting off his dreams. He is making the music he was placed on the planet to make.

For Jack Baker, life comes by way of spinning new melodies, drenching the night with rich harmony, playing the depths of his soul in a way that others can sing along, even without words. Jazz musicians understand this. They don't discuss it much, but they frequently have the experience. When the music is flowing freely, when the rhythm is infectious, they experience the ecstasy that lifts people out of all wretchedness and the joy that mends broken souls. Who wouldn't want to be part of such moments?

Erroll Garner is a musician I discovered early—back when one of the record companies had a subscription plan that began with the offer of a dozen records for a few dollars. In the plan's catalog, I saw a new Garner album and ordered it. It was completely enchanting. In some ways, it seemed a throwback to an earlier age. His left hand pounded out the chords, four to a measure. His ballads were a bit too rhapsodic for my taste. But, wow, could he swing!

A short man who sat on a city telephone book when he played the piano, Erroll's hands flew around the keyboard. He turned toward the audience with a broad smile, playing octave melodies with ease, never looking down to see what he was doing. Most astonishing, he never learned to read written music, often quipping, "Nobody can hear you read."

In a documentary on Garner's life and music, the dancer Maurice Hines said, "The thing that attracted me to Erroll Garner was the joy. He played with such joy that it transmitted to me emotionally. When he started to play, I remember being happy."

Joy. That word keeps coming up, even in sadness.

In May 2013, as thousands gathered at Dave Brubeck's memorial service in the Cathedral of Saint John the Divine, New York, Dave's widow, Iola, stood to greet the crowd. She thanked those who had written the countless letters she had received from around the world since Dave's death five months before. "I noticed that one word—*joy*—kept coming into those letters over and over," Iola said. "They expressed the deep joy his music brought to their lives."

Joy may be the secret revelation at the heart of jazz. Joy builds bridges and creates understanding. Joy melts fear and directs us toward ethical action. Joy sustains us when we have no other human capacity to keep going. Joy is the great mystical gift of music. It is evidence that the Holy Spirit is in the thick of it all.

I wonder if this may be one reason some people shy away from jazz. They are afraid of joy. They are fearful that it might affect them, that it might demand more attention than they planned to give it, that it might free them from the fundamentalism of the printed page, that it might raise *them* from the dead. "The Lord is the Spirit, and where the Spirit of the Lord is, there is freedom," wrote the apostle Paul.

Great freedom. Deep joy. It can come very directly in the making—and hearing—of music.

That's something Barry Ulanov knew. Ulanov was a well-known music critic and editor of the jazz journal *Metronome*. After converting to Catholicism, he became a college professor, teaching at Princeton, Columbia, and Barnard College. A Renaissance man, his academic interest was the intersection of religion and psychology. He also wrote extensively on jazz, publishing an early biography of Duke Ellington, as well as a study of the psychology of Carl Jung.

The story goes that someone once asked him about his two great passions, jazz and the spiritual life. The person asked, "What is their connection?"

He responded with one word: "Ecstasy."

LISTENING

If you, like me, are a listener, you may know firsthand what music can do for us, within us, and among us. It can bring us alive, as with the real-life parable of Rhoda, a woman who belonged to the first church I served.

When Rhoda went to the nursing home, nobody ever thought she would walk again. She spent her days watching game shows and soap operas, an endless cycle of *Wheel of Fortune* and *General Hospital*. She could hardly move down the hall to the television. When she got there, she strained to see the screen. Everyone assumed the end was near.

One day, the activity director announced, "Rhoda, we're going on a bus trip."

Rhoda said, "I don't want to miss my TV shows."

The activity director said, "Don't worry. We'll be back in plenty of time." She wasn't being completely honest, but it got Rhoda on the bus. They put Rhoda's walker by her side, although nobody thought she would use it.

Soon the bus carried Rhoda to a huge arts and music festival in a nearby city. Attendance at the festival that day numbered over one hundred thousand people. It was an ambitious task to take twenty-five nursing home residents to a place like that. It was also a nerve-wracking experience when the activities director counted twenty-four heads at the end of the day. Rhoda was missing.

They looked high and low. They couldn't find her. In time, they located her aluminum walker near a bandstand in a circus tent but no Rhoda.

Suddenly, someone spotted her. Thirty feet away, she was dancing with a man half her age.

"Rhoda!" shouted the director. "What are you doing?"

Rhoda said, "It's the polka!"

"But what about your legs?"

Rhoda shouted back, "When I heard the music, I couldn't stop my toes from tapping."

She was so caught up in the dance, the life-giving dance, that she forgot the limitations that hemmed her in. She heard the music and met a glimpse of the life of eternity—how life, through grace, breaks in here and now.

That's the music of eternity, a new song beyond all we could ever dream or hope. Perhaps we hear it now only in snatches. But when we do, it has the power to leave the aluminum walker behind, getting us on our feet, setting us free.

TESTIFYING!

A few years ago, I had the gift of a summer sabbatical with the primary purpose of exploring music as a holy gift. During an eight-day stretch, I enjoyed about twenty concerts. One musician after another infused my soul with joy.

Among the musicians was African guitarist Lionel Loueke, who improvised in wild time signatures. Saxophonist Donny McCaslin hurled gravity-defying melodies into the air and created musical tornadoes. Then there was Chicago bluesman Buddy Guy, who played his audience like a guitar, barking out exhortations about justice and winking with a smile. Arturo Sandoval blew hair-raising lines on his trumpet and repeated them an octave higher. The Preservation Hall Jazz Band then raised the dead to their feet and made us dance.

It was during this summer that I spent some time with Bobby McFerrin, as described earlier in this book. One morning, he spoke to us of the healing power of music. He shared that the compliment he most wants to hear from a listener after one of his concerts is "I feel so good, so much better than when I came tonight." Why? Because it is the answer to the prayer he offers before every concert: "Lord, let the music help somebody who came with a burden. Let the music heal and lift them."

Music *is* that prayer. It is the ending that has no end. This music has evoked joy in my spirit, and I have witnessed what it can do in others. I am convinced that if we can welcome what jazz offers—with joy, truth, inclusion, and well-being for all—we can be revived, and our common life will flourish.

As theologian Lesslie Newbigin notes, the first mark of the life of the Spirit in a dangerous, dreary, postmodern world is a community of joyful praise. This is "its most distinctive character. Praise is an activity which is almost totally absent from 'modern' society." When joy breaks out, "people find their true freedom, their true dignity, and their true equality in reverence to One who is worthy of all the praise that we can offer."

This is the promise of the spiritual life. We remember there is no prior claim on our lives, no other Voice that requires our attention, no other Lover who deserves our devotion. In my favorite paraphrase of the ancient Psalm 100, "All people that on earth do dwell, sing to the Lord with cheerful voice; Him serve with mirth." Mirth, indeed.

The spiritual life begins and ends with the life-giving joy of the Eternal One. In praise, we cut ourselves loose from the demeaning powers of this age that enslave or destroy. We give ourselves to the God who sets us free and never lets us go.

MOVING TO THE CODA

Where will we hear the far-off hymn that "hails a new creation"?

Sometimes we hear it in a yearning saxophone, trying to participate in the song of the saints. The music may be rough and unfinished. It may never be a complete experience. Yet, for a moment, the musician—and we who listen—get caught up in music much larger than a little bitty tune.

Sometimes we can taste it in a piece of bread or a sip of wine. The church points to its table and says, "This is the banquet of heaven." It is just a taste, of course, as we await the final feast when all people are fed and satisfied. Yet, for a moment, eating and drinking make it so.

Sometimes we can encounter it in daily deeds of kindness, in the ordinary person who protects the weak, feeds the hungry, or embraces the stranger. These good deeds are never complete or finished. There is always more work to do than we can ever accomplish. But we do what we can. God willing, our work is joined to God's work.

So, my friends, let our music be caught up with God's music until the day when every person is fed and satisfied.

When every tear is wiped away.

When every voice is raised in the sound of freedom.

When every broken heart is mended and filled with joy.

IMPROVISATION: ARE YOU GOING TO TALK ABOUT HEAVEN?

The thin, grizzled drummer
removes cymbals
from their stands.
A curious soul, he asks:
So you are writing a book?
What is it about?

I pause to consider
how to condense all these pages
into thirty seconds of attention.
Abundant life does not fit
neatly in an instrument case.

Stepping into my fermata
he asked fervently,
"Are you going to talk
about heaven?"

What can we say of heaven,
God's domain?

Is it the period on the paragraph,
the *fine* on the tune?
Or is it a comma within eternity?
Is heaven flooded with color-blind justice?
Is everybody healed?
Will hungry musicians eat after the gig?

Here is what I know:
Heaven is a jazz solo
sweeping all in its wake.
Every foot taps
every head nods
every soul leans forward,
and nobody wants it to end.

Eyes glistening,
he hears the music.

GLOSSARY OF JAZZ TERMS

Bebop is a style of jazz that emerged as the big bands of the Swing Era declined and World War II began. The tempos sped up, dissonance increased, and musicians played competitively for themselves. Historically, jazz began to lose a good share of its popular audience as bebop began.

Blues is a technical description of a twelve-measure tune that cycles through a standardized sequence of chords. Jazz musicians may complicate the harmonies, but the essence of the blues lies close to the heart of jazz.

Bluesy is an inexact but familiar description of music that has a tongue-curling, soulful quality.

Call and response is an interactive form where a statement is offered and a response is given. Prevalent in the music of Africa, it transcends many cultures. Call and response appeared in the "lining out" of unaccompanied singing, where the leader sang a phrase that the assembly echoed (see the description of psalm singing in chapter 9). It became a defining characteristic of African American preaching as well as gospel-flavored jazz.

Changes refer to chord changes that undergird a tune. "The changes" refer to the repeated sequence of chords in a tune as they occur in real time.

Chords are clusters of note combinations that frequently derive from a scale (see Scales). If based on a scale, they express the essential sound of that scale and suggest possible notes to use in improvisation for that chord's duration.

Contrafact signifies a new melody built on an existing tune and its harmonic structure.

Form refers to the structure of a tune and its performance. At its simplest expression, a tune's form is often repeated in a cycle, providing the soloist with a harmonic map for creating an improvisation.

Gig is an abbreviation for a musical engagement. It is usually an occasion when music is performed in exchange for money, although there are rare occasions when musicians are not paid. It's still a gig.

Hang is short for "hanging out." Often treated as a noun, as in the musician's question, "Where's the hang?"

Improvisation is spontaneous composition. Improvising uses the same imaginative process as composing but is accelerated and unedited.

Jazz has often been described as a musical style, a category for selling recordings, or a suspicious cacophony that frightens church organists and enervates symphony violinists. *Jazz* describes music that blurs any distinction between composition and improvisation. Therefore, jazz can be understood as a verb, not merely a noun.

Modes—see Scales.

Motive (or motif) is a simple building block of melody, perhaps two, three, or four notes. The motive could be repeated, altered, played backward or upside down, or temporarily moved to another scale.

Riff is a short musical phrase, often repeated. The familiar big-band tune "In the Mood" is based on a riff that is played (and slightly altered) three times.

Scales are sequences of unduplicated notes, frequently seven or eight notes. To some listeners, they suggest different moods; for instance, some hear a major scale as happy and a minor scale as sad. The harmony of the medieval church derived from displacements of the major scale, which were named as *modes*. Other scales are developed from micro patterns of intervals, such as the diminished scale or whole tone scale, or artificially constructed to capture a particular sound, such as the blues scale. Chords are frequently based on three or more notes from a scale. As jazz harmony has developed with the art form, chords have grown more complicated.

Solo is a musician's creative expression during the performance of a tune. It can be based on the simple form of the tune or might be an improvised section within a larger composition.

Swing is another indescribable quality in jazz, marked by a strong pulse and forward movement. Swinging music has a groove to it. It invites listeners and musicians to engage physically through tapping feet and hands, nodding the head in rhythm, and dancing.

Syncopation is the displacement of an expected rhythm, often with an intoxicating effect. In the development of jazz, syncopation first became prevalent in ragtime (short for *ragged time*), as eighth notes were combined in unexpected ways.

Tension and release are two tools for musical construction. As with the plot of a story, tension is built through complication—in harmony or rhythm—and then relieved ("released") by resolution. For example, an increasingly dense harmony can suddenly simplify, or a complex rhythm can resolve.

"Thriving on a Riff" is the alternative title of the bebop tune "Anthropology." Composed by Charlie Parker and/or John Birks "Dizzy" Gillespie, it is a contrafact of George Gershwin's "I've Got Rhythm."

Transcribing is the process of listening to notes in the air and putting them on paper. A fundamental process for learning the depths of jazz composition and improvisation, transcription trains the ear to hear subtleties of melody and rhythm. It also provides the brain with a tool for musical analysis.

RECOMMENDED RECORDINGS

Here is a sampling of notable jazz recordings by musicians mentioned in this book. Listening to music is a highly subjective activity, but these recordings represent some of the finest work by these artists. Live recordings are highly recommended and denoted by an asterisk (*).

Louis Armstrong
Plays W. C. Handy
Chet Baker
Chet Baker Sings
*Chet Baker in Tokyo**
Bix Beiderbecke
Singing the Blues
Bob Brookmeyer
*Live at Sandy's Jazz Revival, 1978**
*Live at the Village Vanguard, with Mel Lewis and the Jazz Orchestra**
Dave Brubeck
Dave Digs Disney
Time Out
*At Carnegie Hall**
The Real Ambassadors
John Coltrane
Blue Train
A Love Supreme
Ascension

RECOMMENDED RECORDINGS

Miles Davis
Kind of Blue
In Person: Friday and Saturday Nights at the Blackhawk*

Duke Ellington
Ellington at Newport 1956*
Second Sacred Concert

Bill Evans
Portrait in Jazz
The Paris Concert*

Béla Fleck
Live at the Quick*

Jan Garbarek
Officium
Dresden: In Concert*

Erroll Garner
Concert by the Sea*

Jimmy Greene
Beautiful Life
Flowers—Beautiful Life, Volume 2

Vince Guaraldi
The Grace Cathedral Concert*
A Charlie Brown Christmas

Tord Gustavsen
The Ground
Being There

Herbie Hancock
Speak Like a Child
V.S.O.P. The Quintet*

W. C. Handy
W. C. Handy's Memphis Blues Band

Billie Holiday
20th Century Masters: Best of Billie Holiday

Keith Jarrett
The Koln Concert*
The Melody at Night, with You

Dave Liebman
  *Expansions Live**
  Circular Dreaming
Charles Lloyd
  *Forest Flower**
  Lift Every Voice and Sing
Sherrie Maricle
  Live at Jazz at Lincoln Center's Dizzy's Club Coca-Cola
    (with the Diva Big Band)*
  I Love to See You Smile (with the 3D Jazz Trio)
Wynton Marsalis
  *Live at the Village Vanguard**
  The Abyssinian Mass
Lyle Mays
  *The Ludwigsburg Concert**
  Lyle Mays
Bobby McFerrin
  Spirityouall
  Bang! Zoom
Pat Metheny
  *Travels**
  *The Road to You**
Charles Mingus
  Mingus Ah Um
Thelonious Monk
  *Big Band and Quartet in Concert**
  *With John Coltrane at Carnegie Hall**
Lee Morgan
  *Live at the Lighthouse**
  Night Dreamer (with Wayne Shorter)
Jelly Roll Morton
  Birth of the Hot: The Classic Chicago "Red Hot Peppers"
    Sessions 1926–27
Charlie Parker
  *The Quintet: Live at Massey Hall**

Best of the Complete Savoy and Dial Studio Recordings
Gary Peacock
Standards (with Keith Jarrett)
At the Blue Note (with Keith Jarrett)*
Bud Powell
The Amazing Bud Powell
Willie Ruff
Breaking the Silence: Standards, Strayhorn, and Lullabies
Lalo Schifrin
Latin Jazz Suite
Clark Terry
*Live on QE 2**
*Clark Terry's Big B-A-D Band Live**
McCoy Tyner
*Enlightenment: Live at Montreux**
Thomas "Fats" Waller
The Very Best of Fats Waller
Kenny Werner
*Live at Maybeck**
Unprotected Music
Mary Lou Williams
*Live at the Cookery**
Mary Lou's Mass (Smithsonian Folkways)
Phil Woods
*Live at the Showboat**
*Live at the Deer Head Inn**
Yellowjackets
Blue Hats
*Mint Jam**

ACKNOWLEDGMENTS

Over the thirty years this book has gestated, I have developed a list of people to thank.

As the first person to introduce me to music, my mother, Elizabeth Ann ("Betsy"), leads the list. Thank you for the musical DNA, the taste for Basie, and the Armstrong ticket from 1955. I'm glad to report the piano lessons worked out.

My late father, Glenn, drove me to my first jazz gig (a Mormon youth dance that paid fifteen dollars for three hours). He heard me sing "Moon River" for the first and last time and told my sister not to laugh.

My late grandmother, Isabella ("Ebo") Stewart, gleefully corrupted me with two Dave Brubeck LPs and cheered when Dave and I became friends.

Thanks to Bobby McFerrin, Dave Brubeck, Bob Brookmeyer, Dave Liebman, Sherrie Maricle, Phil Woods, Mike Holober, Deanna Witkowski, Bill Mays, Donny McCaslin, and countless other jazz musicians who have befriended me in the living tradition that is our lifeblood.

Special thanks to Willie Ruff, who kept me in stitches during a conversation I'll never forget; and Chuck Marohnic, who spoke from the depths of his very deep spirit.

My mentor, Al Hamme, feared I would never return to the stage when I went off to the far country of Princeton Theological Seminary, yet he welcomed me back when I did. Al helped me form the rest of the Presbybop Music family: Tony Marino, Ron Vincent, Mike Carbone, Jeff Stockham, Steve Gilmore, Tom Whaley, and all the cats who have subbed for them. They are my brothers.

Special thanks to Presbybop assistants Jan Thyren and Jamie Strong and to the multitalented Jeff Kellam. They make things happen and chase the details I cannot see.

The late Thomas W. Gillespie, president of Princeton Theological Seminary, provided deep encouragement for me to integrate my pastoral and musical gifts when others thought it should be an either/or decision.

Bill Pindar, Clown for Jesus, ripped open a locked piano lid at Old Pine Church to hear me play and has kept the friendship fire burning for thirty-five years. He saw the connections before I did and helped me bring Dave Brubeck to our first Jazz and the Church Conference.

Carl Wilton and Claire Pula offered us a writing cabin in the Adirondacks, and Nancy Phillips offered Nancy's-by-the-Sea in Warwick, Rhode Island. Both are beautiful and peaceful spots to compose words, reflecting their generous souls and gracious spirits.

Dr. Lia Richards-Palmiter provided me with a writing office on the third floor of the Library and Learning Commons at Marywood University, Scranton, Pennsylvania. What a tremendous gift!

Thanks to the Feedback Squad, who read the manuscript and offered incisive suggestions to improve it: jazz historian Derrick Bang, theologian Brent Eelman, spiritual director Diane Stephens Hogue, jazz radio host and church educator Jeff Kellam, legit musician Dr. Susan Kelly, and Presbybop superfan Alvin Stenzel.

To my clear-eyed editors, Lil Copan and Corey McCullough, who saw what I did not and suggested the necessary repairs.

The people of my beloved congregation, the First Presbyterian Church of Clarks Summit, Pennsylvania, have been my partners in ministry and music-making since December 1990. They granted me two sabbaticals to explore music as a spiritual practice and a third sabbatical to write this book.

Dr. Terry Singer is the guy who stood up at the back of the Clarks Summit church to say, "We heard you preach, but could you play us something on the piano?" He is a special saint of God despite his objections to this attribution. He's also a purveyor of fine bourbon.

The Louisville Institute provided the Pastoral Study Project grant that funded my research and writing. Special thanks to Rev. Dr. Edwin Aponte, former director, and Rev. Don Richter, former associate director, as well as Rev. Dr. Sheldon Sorge and Rev. Dr. Brent Eelman for their strong support for initiating this project.

The Brubeck Institute and Archives, formerly housed at the Holt-Atherton Special Collections, University of the Pacific, Stockton, California, provided a generous study grant to spend a week researching Dave's work and correspondence. Mike Wurtz and Nicole Grady Mountjoy provided invaluable research assistance.

The Presbytery of Lackawanna (PCUSA) and moderator Wayne Wolfe provided a generous sabbatical grant. It allowed for the necessary pastoral coverage during my time away to pray, listen, think, write, and edit.

I offer my highest praise and deepest thanks to my household, presided over by my beloved life partner, Jamie Strong, and including our son, Josh, and our daughters, Lauren, Katie, and Meg. They have given love and support beyond measure. They keep me honest. When I watch jazz videos on the TV, they mistake them for commercials on the Weather Channel.

Over the years, portions of this material have been shared with the wonderful people of Stony Point Center, Stony Point, New York; Ghost Ranch, Abiquiu, New Mexico; Princeton Theological Seminary, Princeton, New Jersey; Pittsburgh Theological Seminary, Pittsburgh, Pennsylvania; Bay View Association, Petoskey, Michigan; Epworth Assembly, Ludington, Michigan; Chautauqua Institution, Chautauqua, New York; Kirkridge Retreat Center, Bangor, Pennsylvania; Massanetta Springs Conference Center, Harrisonburg, Virginia; the Cathedral Church of St. James, Toronto, Ontario; Freemason Street Baptist Church, Norfolk, Virginia; Day 1 radio ministry, Atlanta, Georgia; Association of Partners in Christian Education, meeting all over the place; Festival of Homiletics, held in Washington, DC, and Atlanta, Georgia; and countless churches where I have made music and talked way too much.

PERMISSIONS

"What Is Contemplation" by Thomas Merton, from *New Seeds of Contemplation*, © 1961 by The Abbey of the Gethsemane, Inc. Reprinted by permission of New Directions Publishing Corp.

"The Popular Definitions of Improvisation" by Paul F. Berliner, from *Thinking in Jazz: The Infinite Art of Improvisation*, © 1994. Permission conveyed through Copyright Clearance Center, Inc.

"The Great Spiritual Call" by Henri J. M. Nouwen, from *Life of the Beloved: Spiritual Living in a Secular World*, © 1992. Reprinted by arrangement with The Crossroad Publishing Company, www.crossroadpublishing.com.

"They Say I Look Like God," lyrics by Dave and Iola Brubeck, © 1962. Renewed 1990; Derry Music Company. All rights reserved.

NOTES

INTRODUCTION

"The glory of God is a human alive": Irenaeus, *Adversus haereses* (*Against Heresies*), Book IV, chapter 20, paragraph 7. Available online at https://ccel.org/ccel/schaff/anf01/anf01/Page_490.html.

CHAPTER ONE

L'Engle writes, "We are afraid of the Transfiguration": Madeleine L'Engle, *Walking on Water: Reflections on Faith and Art* (Wheaton, IL: Harold Shaw, 1980), 80–81.

When we started the gig that night: Christian McBride, post on Facebook, March 6, 2020, https://www.facebook.com/officialchristianmcbride/posts/pfbid0Ro7so7iA4ZhUzKNPkhctaQYNpkDbhNAYeSjNesr7YvCDpNi9qnqZYQXTYLc9EWHhl.

"I'm not sure": McBride, Facebook, March 6, 2020.

"This gig wasn't simply a gig": McBride, Facebook, March 6, 2020.

After that you shall come to Gibeath-elohim: 1 Samuel 10:5–7, NRSV.

When the music began, I knew I was going to witness: Personal correspondence with Catherine Azar, reminiscing after the death of Lyle Mays, February 15, 2020.

No full itinerary of that week exists: Personal correspondence, July 2020. For more on this period of Armstrong's career, see Ricky Riccardi, *What a Wonderful World* (New York: Pantheon, 2011).

When you're playing and you're in control: Personal conversation, March 6, 2012, Mount Pocono, Pennsylvania.

I had never in my life heard music like that: I have heard Mr. McFerrin tell this account many times. This version comes from "So the Story Goes: Bobby McFerrin's Fateful Night in Hollywood," *Jazz Stories* on Jazz at Lincoln Center Radio, July 27, 2017, Transcript available at https://www.jazz.org/blog/so-the-story-goes-bobby-mcferrins-fateful-night-in-hollywood/.

When he traveled to Louisville for medical appointments: Robert Weldon
Whalen, "Thomas Merton and John Coltrane: Jazz and the Mercy beyond
Being" (presented at the 15th Biannual Meeting of the International Thomas
Merton Society, at St. Bonaventure University, New York, June 15–18, 2017).
The club on Washington Street was located directly across the street from
the building where the Presbyterian Church (USA) currently has its national
offices.

As Merton explains, contemplation is: Thomas Merton, *New Seeds for Contemplation* (New York: New Directions Publishing, 1971), 1–2.

CHAPTER TWO

***Jazz is a music in which the line between composition and performance is
blurred:*** Hugh J. Roberts, "Improvisation, Individuation, and Immanence:
Thelonious Monk," *Black Sacred Music* 3, no. 2 (Fall 1989): 50–56.

It was more about entertainment than accuracy: For those who wish to learn
more, I recommend *Jazz*, a monumental PBS television miniseries in 2001
by Ken Burns.

"I pay you guys": Herbie Hancock, "Four Lessons in Innovation from
Jazz Master Miles Davis," American Masters (PBS), Season 34, Episode 1, https://www.pbs.org/wnet/americanmasters/four-lessons-in
-innovation-from-jazz-great-miles-davis/13460/.

"Don't play what's there": Paul Tingen, *Miles Beyond: Electric Explorations
of Miles Davis, 1967–1991* (New York: Billboard Books, 2001), 1, https://
miles-beyond.com/ch1.htm.

"Don't play the butter notes": Herbie Hancock, *Possibilities* (New York: Viking,
2014), 65.

"It's like a curse": Miles Davis, quoted in *The Washington Post*, March 13,
1969.

One night, my jazz quartet finished a concert: This was Grandma Ebo, the
same grandmother who introduced me to the music of Dave Brubeck.

He left listeners scratching their heads: See Mark 6:2, NRSV.

Webster's Dictionary holds that "to improvise is to compose": *Webster's
New World Dictionary*, 3rd college ed. (New York: Simon and Schuster,
1988).

The popular definitions of improvisation: Paul F. Berliner, *Thinking in Jazz:
The Infinite Art of Improvisation* (Chicago: University of Chicago Press,
1994), 492.

"Every time he plays": Personal conversation with Albert P. Hamme, Binghamton University, March 1980.

"O sing to the Lord": Psalm 96:1, NRSV.

For a long time I have held my peace: Isaiah 42:14, NRSV.

I will lead the blind: Isaiah 42:16, NRSV.

"It took that long to get it all in": Cuthbert Ormond Simpkins, *Coltrane: A Biography* (Baltimore: Black Classic Press, 1977), 76.

"Take the horn out of your mouth": Bill Crow, *Jazz Anecdotes* (New York: Oxford University Press, 1990), 324–325.

It sounded heavenly: J. C. Thomas, *Chasing the Trane* (New York: Da Capo, 1976), 87.

"If we listen to the singing": Walter Brueggemann, "Disciplines of Readiness," Dedication of the Presbyterian Center, Presbyterian Church (USA), Louisville, KY, October 28, 1988.

CHAPTER THREE

Jazz music was invented by demons for the torture of imbeciles: Henry Van Dyke, in a speech to the National Educational Association. Reported in *New York Herald Tribune*, February 28, 1921.

The text chosen for the sermon: See Luke 15:11–32, NRSV.

"Does Jazz Put the Sin in Syncopation?": Anne Shaw Faulkner, "Does Jazz Put the Sin in Syncopation?," *Ladies Home Journal* 38 (August 1921): 16–34, http://arcadiasystems.org/academia/syncopate.html.

As I understand it, it is not music at all: Faulkner, "Does Jazz Put the Sin in Syncopation?"

The namesake of Saint John's African Orthodox Church: Visit the congregation's website at https://www.coltranechurch.org/.

If, however, average listeners hear a masterwork: A subtle nod to the character of Emperor Joseph II in the film *Amadeus* (1984), directed by Milos Forman and adapted by Peter Shaffer from his play.

Accounts of what happened next differ: Jamie Howison, *God's Mind in That Music: Theological Explorations through the Music of John Coltrane* (Eugene, OR: Cascade, 2012), 67–72.

During the year 1957: John Coltrane, liner notes to *A Love Supreme*, Impulse! AS-77.

The sloppy eighth notes from his final recordings: Compare, for instance, "Trane's Blues" with the Miles Davis Quintet (May 11, 1956) with his own recording of "Blue Train" (September 15, 1957).

Heaven is my throne: Isaiah 66:1, NRSV.

"God made one world, not two": Quoted by Deanna Witkowski, from an interview, April 2009, www.deannajazz.com. Link for interview: http://www.urbanfaith.com/2009/04/a-chanteuse-of-sacred-jazz.html.

"You may be an undigested bit of beef": Charles Dickens, *A Christmas Carol* (New York: Bantam, 1986), 14.

Christ took upon himself this human form: Dietrich Bonhoeffer, *The Cost of Discipleship* (New York: Touchstone, 1995), 301.

"What has come into being": John 1:3–4, NRSV.

CHAPTER FOUR

Now that I think about it: Keith Jarrett, "Inside Out: Thoughts on Free Playing," in *Horizons Touched*, ed. Steve Lake and Paul Griffiths (London: Granta, 2007), 239.

"Upon this rock, I will build": Matthew 16:18.

And when the moment came: From a personal conversation in October 1999, Stony Point Center, Stony Point, NY.

"Either that, or he's trying": Personal conversation, October 1999. See also the oral history project available from University of the Pacific, Brubeck's alma mater, https://scholarlycommons.pacific.edu/bohp/31/.

Dr. Pederson compares God to a jazz musician: Ann Pederson, *God, Creation, and All That Jazz: A Process of Composition and Improvisation* (St. Louis: Chalice, 2001), 15–28.

Six syllables, an incomplete sentence: Stanley Dance, *The World of Duke Ellington* (New York: Charles Scribner's Sons, 1970), 253.

They call it "the jazz factor": David F. Ford and Daniel W. Hardy, *Living in Praise: Worshipping and Knowing God*, rev. ed. (Grand Rapids, MI: Baker Academic, 2005), 26, 159.

"My Father is still working": John 5:17.

That posse of authoritarians knew: Michael Kater, *Different Drummers: Jazz in the Culture of Nazi Germany* (New York: Oxford University Press, 1992).

The idiocy of the entire Christian world: Dave Brubeck, liner notes, *The Light in the Wilderness: An Oratorio for Today*, Musical Heritage Society 513442A, 1968.

"Love your enemies": Luke 6:27.

Though certain, as (Bergman) said: Michael Tucker, "Northbound: ECM and 'The Idea of True North,'" in *Horizons Touched*, ed. Steve Lake and Paul Griffiths (London: Granta, 2007), 31.

"God above God": Paul Tillich, *The Courage to Be* (New Haven, CT: Yale University Press, 2000), 190.

Jazz answered needs that traditional faiths did not: Neil Leonard, *Jazz: Myth and Religion* (New York: Oxford University Press, 1987), 178.

When Hancock retold this story in his Noble Lectures at Harvard University: Herbie Hancock tells the story online in "The Ethics of Jazz," 2014 Noble Lectures, Harvard University, https://youtu.be/EPFXC3q1tTg.

CHAPTER FIVE

Your intuition and your intellect: Madeleine L'Engle, quoted in Mhaly Csikszentmihalyi, *Creativity: Flow and the Psychology of Discovery and Invention* (New York: Harper Perennial, reprint ed., 2013), 239.

"Never forget": Tim Harford, "How Frustration Can make Us more Creative," https://www.ted.com/talks/tim_harford_how_frustration _can_make_us_more_creative/transcript.

One observer of the Koln concert identifies: Peter Elsdon, *Keith Jarrett's The Koln Concert: Oxford Studies in Recorded Jazz* (New York: Oxford University Press, 2012), 82.

People stood up and cheered: David Hajdu, "Wynton's Blues," *Atlantic Monthly*, March 2003, https://www.theatlantic.com/magazine /archive/2003/03/wyntons-blues/302684/.

Keith Jarrett had been handed a mess: Tim Harford, "How Frustration Can Make Us More Creative," TED Talk, September 2015, https://www .ted.com/talks/tim_harford_how_frustration_can_make_us_more _creative?language=en.

We can experience this through simple games: MaryAnn McKibben Dana, *God, Improv, and the Art of Living* (Grand Rapids, MI: Wm. B. Eerdmans, 2018), 9–58.

"What makes experiences in life genuinely satisfying": Mihaly Csikszentmihalyi, *Flow: The Psychology of Optimal Experiences* (New York: Harper Perennial, 1990).

"When I drop my hands on the piano": Kenny Werner, *Effortless Mastery: Freeing the Master Musician Within* (New Albany, IN: Jamey Aebersold Jazz, 1996), 91.

At the same time, the part of the brain: Katrina Schwartz, "Creativity and the Brain: What We Can Learn from Jazz Musicians," MindShift, April 11, 2014, http://ww2.kqed.org/mindshift/2014/04/11/the -link-between-jazz-improvisation-and-student-creativity/.

"where the brain meets the soul": Pat Metheny, Keynote Speech, Society for Neuroscience Conference, November 3, 2018. Transcription at https://dana. org/article/sfn18-pat-metheny-at-dialogues-lecture/.

To me, that's the glue: Metheny, Keynote Speech.

The Lord created me at the beginning: Proverbs 8:22–25, NRSV.

"When God marked the foundations": Proverbs 8:30–31, NRSV.

First, the music enters us: Gary Peacock, quoted in "Keith Jarrett: The Art of Improvisation," DVD, Alliance, 2005.

Music will happen according to: Bob Brookmeyer, quoted in Rob Hudson, *Evolution: The Improvisational Style of Bob Brookmeyer* (Vienna: Universal Edition, 2002), v.

For whoever finds me: Proverbs 8:35–36, NRSV.

"But if the musician isn't honest": David Friesen, "The Christian Musicians: Lecture 2," Online lecture, www.davidfriesen.net, 9:07–10:08.

"The imagination is among the chief": Eugene Peterson, "Masters of Imagination," in *Subversive Spirituality* (Grand Rapids, MI: Wm. B. Eerdmans, 1997), 133–134.

"I want to be a force for real good": John Coltrane to Frank Kofsky, *Coltrane on Coltrane: The Coltrane Interviews* (Chicago: Chicago Review Press, 2012).

CHAPTER SIX

Bix's tone was so pure: Terry Teachout, "Homage to Bix," *Commentary: The Monthly Magazine of Opinion*, September 2005, https://www.commentary.org/articles/terry-teachout/homage-to-bix/.

"When I fall in love": "When I Fall in Love," music by Victor Young, lyrics by Edward Heyman.

"toward the full realization": Henri J. M. Nouwen, *Life of the Beloved: Spiritual Living in a Secular World* (New York: Crossroad Publishing, 1992), 96.

The great spiritual call of the Beloved Children: Nouwen, *Life of the Beloved*, 97–98.

"like reaching for smoke": This is a good translation of the Hebrew word for *vanity*. See Eugene H. Peterson, *The Message* (Colorado Springs, CO: NavPress, 2002), 1164.

I hit a wall: Dorothy Darr, *Charles Lloyd: Arrows into Infinity* (Munich: ECM Records, 2012).

"Lloyd's largesse here is his sincerity": https://www.allaboutjazz.com/lift-every-voice-charles-lloyd-ecm-records-review-by-mark-corroto.php.

"I was telling the disease": Quoted in "Keith Jarrett: The Art of Improvisation."

"If you looked away": Peter Pettinger, *Bill Evans: How My Heart Sings* (New Haven, CT: Yale University Press, 1998), 145.

"When he came down": Pettinger, *Bill Evans*, 62.

Or painkillers. Or cocaine: See Miles Davis with Quincy Troupe, *Miles: The Autobiography* (New York: Simon and Schuster, 1989), 169–170, 326–327, 345–341.

"like pearls falling": Jim Cullum Jr., "Bix Beiderbecke." Accessed June 1, 2023, http://atjs.org/Bixbeiderbecke.html.

"Beiderbecke took out": Brendan Wolfe, *Finding Bix: The Life and Afterlife of a Jazz Legend* (Iowa City: University of Iowa Press, 2017), 137.

Then one day, still in his bathrobe: As reported by Geoffrey C. Ward, *Jazz: A History of America's Music* (New York: Knopf, 2002), 155.

"We have this treasure in clay jars": 2 Corinthians 4:7.

"Please don't mention we said anything": Richard M. Sudhalter and Philip R. Evans, *Bix: Man and Legend* (New Rochelle, NY: Arlington House, 1974), 327.

CHAPTER SEVEN

God helps people through jazz: From an interview in 1978, in Lowell D. Holmes and John W. Thomson, *Jazz Greats: Getting Better with Age* (New York: Holmes and Meier, 1986).

I don't even remember how it all got started: The account comes from an interview on NPR, https://www.npr.org/2013/12/14/250786728 /a-grieving-newtown-mothers-motto-love-wins.

"Music is extremely helpful": Philip Lutz, "Years after Newtown Massacre, a Father Plays through the Pain," *New York Times,* August 26, 2016, https:// www.nytimes.com/2016/08/28/nyregion/years-after-newtown-massacre-a -father-plays-through-the-pain.html.

"I still think of my little girl": Lutz, "Years after Newtown Massacre."

The importance of the blues: Father Peter O'Brien, SJ, "Mary Lou Williams: Jazz for the Soul," *Smithsonian Folkways Magazine,* Fall 2010, https://folkways.si.edu/magazine-fall-2010-mary-lou-williams-jazz-soul /ragtime/music/article/smithsonian.

One of them encouraged her: Michael Scott Alexander, "The Conversion of Mary Lou Williams," *America Magazine,* February 2021, 54–58.

Parker's death symbolized: Tammy L. Kernodle, *Soul on Soul: The Life and Music of Mary Lou Williams* (Boston: Northeastern University Press, 2004), 167–177.

"YOUR ATTENTIVE PARTICIPATION": O'Brien, "Mary Lou Williams."

*It was his expert, evocative string-playing:*1 Samuel 16:14–23.

"With Bach," he wrote, "there is always a message": Karl Barth, *Wolfgang Amadeus Mozart* (Grand Rapids, MI: Eerdmans, 1986), 37.

Her angelic voice was simultaneously: Kirk Byron Jones, *The Jazz of Preaching: How to Preach with Great Freedom and Joy* (Nashville: Abingdon Press, 2004), 12.

The album was called Officium: Jan Garbarek, "The Hilliard Ensemble," *Officium,* ECM 1525 NS, 1994.

I have heard so many touching reports: Tord Gustavsen, interview with the Royal College of Psychiatrists, United Kingdom, originally published online at http://www.rcpsych.ac.uk/discoverpsychiatry/blogzone/mindsinmusic /tordgustavseninterview.aspx.

She hit the brother's car: "Tord Gustavsen: Norwegian Deep-Feeling Zone," *Downbeat Magazine,* August 6, 2012.

He played, composed, mourned: Recorded on Tord Gustavsen, *The Ground,* ECM 1892, 2005.

CHAPTER EIGHT

From the biblical scrolls of the First and Second Chronicles: 1 Chronicles 25:1, 6, NRSV.

Their musical accompaniment was deemed a "ministry": 2 Chronicles 7:6, NRSV.

when the song was raised: 2 Chronicles 5:13–14, NRSV.

The battle can even be seen: For instance, see the scripture introductions to Psalm 56 ("To the leader: according to The Dove on Far-off Terebrinth") or Psalm 80 ("To the leader: on Lilies, a Covenant"). These refer to ancient tunes, now lost.

Now that's praying: As reported by Thomas T. Spencer, "Something 'Hot and Abstract': Thomas Merton, Mary Lou Williams and the Spirituality of Jazz," *Merton Seasonal: A Quarterly Review* 43, no. 3 (Fall 2018): 4.

"the exorcism of despair": Albert Murray, *Stomping the Blues,* 40th Anniversary ed. (Minneapolis: University of Minnesota Press, 2017), vii.

One biographer describes how John sat: J. C. Thomas, *Chasin' the Trane: The Music and Mystique of John Coltrane* (New York: Da Capo, 1975), 183–184.

He went into isolation: Alice Coltrane to Branford Marsalis, interview in *Coltrane's A Love Supreme Live in Amsterdam,* Marsalis Music, DVD, 6:20–7:10.

And to this day, A Love Supreme: In addition to countless articles, see Howison, *God's Mind in That Music,* 135–151; Lewis Porter, *John Coltrane: His Life and Music* (Ann Arbor: University of Michigan Press, 1998), 231–249; and the masterwork by Ashley Kahn, *A Love Supreme: The Story of John Coltrane's Signature Album* (New York: Viking, 2002).

Later discovered by his family: View the composition online at https://sova.si.edu/record/NMAH.AC.0903.

He's telling us that God is everywhere: Porter, *John Coltrane: His Life and Music,* 242.

John's band had been working: According to Porter's later research, saxophonist Frank Tiberi recorded Coltrane playing "Resolution" at Pep's, a Philadelphia club, on September 18, 1964, three months before Coltrane recorded the suite. See Lewis Porter, "A Deep Dive into John Coltrane's 'A Love Supreme,'" WBGO-FM, July 20, 2020, https://www.wbgo.org/music/2020-07-17/a-deep-dive-into-john-coltranes-a-love-supreme-by-his-biographer-lewis-porter-pt-1#stream/0.

The text begins with a description: See Porter, "A Deep Dive into John Coltrane's 'A Love Supreme,'" chapter 3.

As time and events moved on: A Love Supreme, liner notes.

His improvised melody: Coltrane's fans post videos regularly on YouTube to combine his words with his improvised melody. As of this writing, here is one version: https://www.youtube.com/watch?v=BmbWRZfOgwc.

"get the original emotional essence of the spiritual": John Coltrane, liner notes, *"Live" at the Village Vanguard,* Impulse A-10, 1961.

They had just concluded a Sunday School lesson: As reported by Thomas, *Chasin' the Trane,* 167.

Not one to take a public stand: Howison, *God's Mind in That Music,* 123.

So they did not die in vain: Martin Luther King Jr., "Eulogy for the Martyred Children," in *A Testament of Hope: The Essential Writings and Speeches of Martin Luther King, Jr.,* ed. James Melvin Washington (New York: Harper-Collins, 1986), 221–223. Lewis Porter has explored the connection between Coltrane's "Alabama" and Dr. King's eulogy in "'They Did Not Die in

Vain': on 'Alabama,' John Coltrane Carefully Wrought Anguish into Grace," broadcast on WBGO-FM, November 18, 2020.

When I listen to Coltrane playing: Ismail Muhammad, "On John Coltrane's 'Alabama,'" *Paris Review*, July 17, 2020, https://www.theparisreview.org /blog/2020/06/17/on-john-coltranes-alabama/.

"It will wreck you": Colin Fleming, "Of George Floyd and John Coltrane: Listening to 'Alabama' in the Days Following a Nation-Shaking Killing," *JazzTimes*, June 2, 2020, https://jazztimes.com/features/columns /of-george-floyd-and-john-coltrane/.

"And when I get the good 'soul'": This is a widely repeated quote. The origin may be "Jazz: The Prayerful One," *Time Magazine*, February 21, 1964, https://content.time.com/time/subscriber/article/0,33009,870827,00 .html.

"Once you become aware of": Quoted by Nat Hentoff in his liner notes for Coltrane's album *Meditations*. From *Coltrane on Coltrane: The John Coltrane Interviews*, ed. Chris DeVito (Chicago: Chicago Review Books, 2010), 263.

CHAPTER NINE

Bird gave the world his music: Phil Woods with Ted Panken, *Life in E Flat: The Autobiography of Phil Woods* (Torrance, CA: Cymbal, 2020), 85.

Through our suffering: Mary Lou Williams, "Has the Black American Musician Lost His Creativeness and Heritage in Jazz?," 1, 4, Series 5: Personal Papers, ca. 1970–1971, Box 2, Folder 25, Mary Lou Williams Collection, Institute of Jazz Studies, Rutgers University.

"You have done me a great injustice": Open letter from Jelly Roll Morton to Robert Ripley, published in *Downbeat Magazine*, August 1938.

"Because of my exceptional ability": The published correspondence is reported by Paul Merry in the blog post "1938 Heavyweight Blues Clash," http:// paulmerryblues.com/2018/12.

A wide variety of people: Harvey Cox, *Fire from Heaven: The Rise of Pentecostal Spirituality and the Reshaping of Religion in the Twenty-First Century* (Reading, MA: Addison-Wesley, 1995), 143–144.

Through all the sorrow: W. E. B. DuBois, *The Souls of Black Folk* (New York: Bantam Classic, 1903), 116.

"I think these spirituals": Quoted in Henry Louis Gates Jr., *The Black Church: This Is Our Story, This Is Our Song* (New York: Penguin, 2021), 69.

"The divine liberation of the oppressed": James Cone, *The Spirituals and the Blues* (New York: Seabury, 1972), 44.

A few years ago, Willie Ruff: Personal conversation, June 3, 2020.

As someone once noted: Gerald Horne, *Jazz and Justice: Racism and the Political Economy of the Music* (New York: Monthly Review Press, 2019), 11, 35.

"The remarkable thing to me": Chuck McCutcheon, "Alabama Choir, Scots Linked by love of Psalm Singing," Newhouse News Service, August 12, 2011.

"Jazz is folk music": Keith Jarrett, interviewed by Kimihiko Yamashita, "In Search of Folk Roots," in *On Music*, ed. Daniel Halpern and Jeanne Wilmot Carter (New York: Ecco, 1994), 114.

"disgraceful intermingling of the races": Ched Myers, "Pentecost, Part 1—Cultural Insurgency and Gospel Liberation: Reflections on Jazz, Pentecostal Faith, and the Church," presented at the 2004 Jazz and the Church Conference, cosponsored by Presbybop Music and the Stony Point Center, https://chedmyers.org/.

forever seeking to overcome oppression: Myers, "Pentecost, Part 1—Cultural Insurgency and Gospel Liberation: Reflections on Jazz, Pentecostal Faith, and the Church."

The truth is, the first great improviser: Donald M. Marquis, *In Search of Buddy Bolden: First Man of Jazz*, rev. ed. (Baton Rouge, LA: Louisiana State University Press, 2005), 30–31.

Louis Armstrong said he heard Buddy play: Louis Armstrong, radio broadcast on the Voice of America, 1956.

"the most powerful trumpet in the world": Matt Micucci, "A Short History of the Legend of Buddy Bolden," *JazzIz*, March 6, 2019, https://www.jazziz.com/a-short-history-of-the-legend-of-buddy-bolden/.

"He was passionate about the music's worth": Willie Ruff, *A Call to Assembly* (New York: Penguin, 1991), 31–32.

I think jazz, no matter what: Keith Jarrett, transcribed from a promotional CD interview with Timothy Hill, ECM DJ-20004-2, 1994.

CHAPTER TEN

Mr. Secretary, my job: Quoted in Walter Brueggemann, *Like Fire in the Bones: Listening for the Prophetic Word in Jeremiah* (Minneapolis: Fortress, 2006), 200.

And they denounced the governor: Charles Mingus, "Original Faubus Fables," © Jazz Workshop, Inc. Lyrics are widely available online. See https://en.wikipedia.org/wiki/Fables_of_Faubus.

"a classic Negro put-down": Don Heckman, "About Charles Mingus," *American Record Guide* (August 1962): 916–918.

"strange fruit hanging": Abel Meeropol, "Strange Fruit," originally published as "Bitter Fruit" in *The New York Teacher*, January 1937. See John M. Carvalho, "Strange Fruit: Music between Violence and Death," *The Journal of Aesthetics and Art Criticism* 71, no. 1 (2013): 111–119.

To nobody's surprise: David Margolick, *Strange Fruit: Billie Holiday, Café Society, and an Early Cry for Civil Rights* (Philadelphia: Running Press, 2000), 61–62.

A faith that began with the atrocity: Galatians 3:13, NRSV.

"Billie Holiday's rendition of 'Strange Fruit'": James H. Cone, *The Cross and the Lynching Tree* (Maryknoll, NY: Orbis, 2011), 134–139.

On July 17, 1959, she died: Johann Hari, "The Hunting of Billie Holiday: How Lady Day Was in the Middle of a Federal Bureau of Narcotics Fight for Survival," *Politico Magazine*, January 17, 2015, https://www.politico.com/magazine/story/2015/01/drug-war-the-hunting-of-billie-holiday-114298/. The story has been dramatized into the film *The United States vs. Billie Holiday*, directed by Lee Daniels (2021).

I hate, I despise your festivals: Amos 5:21–24, NRSV.

"Justice is what love": Cornel West, "Spiritual Blackout, Imperial Meltdown, Prophetic Fightback," Askwith Forum, Harvard Graduate School of Education, October 4, 2017, https://www.youtube.com/watch?v=zuxqhsrCGeg.

It is a decision between: "Geoffrey C. Ward and Wynton Marsalis in conversation at Chautauqua Institution," August 23, 2016, https://wyntonmarsalis.org/videos/view/geoffrey-ward-wynton-marsalis-conversation-chautauqua-institution. Timing: 33:22–34:51.

With this, the college president consented: See Philip Clark, *Dave Brubeck: A Life in Time* (New York: Hachette, 2020), 201–203; Stephen A. Crist, *Dave Brubeck's Time Out: Oxford Studies in Recorded Jazz* (New York: Oxford University Press, 2019), 30–35; Kelsey A. K. Klotz, "Dave Brubeck's Southern Strategy," *Daedalus: The Journal of the American Academy of Arts and Sciences* 48, no. 2 (2019): 52–66.

Then he said to his bass player: Recounted to Hedley Smith, "Dave on the Racial Barrier," http://www.pbs.org/brubeck/talking/daveOnRacial.htm.

There was just one catch: Memo from Bob Bundy to Dave Brubeck, October 6, 1959. Business Correspondence, Brubeck Collection, College of the Pacific. See also Crist, *Dave Brubeck's Time Out*, 228–232.

For Dave, it was a matter: Ralph Gleason, "Concerts Canceled: Racial Issue 'Kills' Brubeck Jazz Tour of the South," *San Francisco Chronicle*, January 12, 1960. Brubeck Collection, College of the Pacific.

"We did the right thing": Personal conversation, Wilton, CT, September 1998.

It is less obvious: Isabel Wilkerson, *Caste: The Origins of Our Discontents* (New York: Random House, 2020).

"Brubeck, your mind's not here": Fred M. Hall, *It's About Time: The Dave Brubeck Story* (Fayetteville: The University of Arkansas Press, 1996), 16–17.

As he reflected on this experience: Smith, "Dave on the Racial Barrier."

But Burns later told Chris: Chris Brubeck, "My Mentor, My Collaborator, My Father: Dave Brubeck," https://nmbx.newmusicusa.org/my-mentor-my-collaborator-my-father-dave-brubeck/.

They say I look like God: Dave Brubeck and Iola Brubeck, "They Say I Look Like God," *The Real Ambassadors*, 1962, Renewed 1990. Derry Music Company. Used by permission.

Because of their long history: Dave Brubeck, liner notes for *The Gates of Justice*, Naxos 8.559414. Text online at http://www.milkenarchive.org/music /volumes/view/swing-his-praises/work/the-gates-of-justice/#linernotes.

"He's important because he stood up": Wynton Marsalis, spoken introduction, "The Life and Music of Dave Brubeck," Jazz at Lincoln Center, New York, April 12, 2014. Concert online at https://www.youtube.com /watch?v=PQ-yXQItCGg.

CHAPTER ELEVEN

A jazz band means: Stanley Crouch, liner notes for Charles Lloyd's album *Jumping the Creek*, ECM 1911, 2005.

"There are more towns in America": Benny Goodman in Nat Shapiro and Nat Hentoff, *Hear Me Talkin' to Ya* (New York: Da Capo, 1979), 317–318.

"I think I saw the Eiffel Tower": Personal conversation, September 5, 1999.

That was my gift: Davis with Troupe, *Miles*, 399.

"Shared art-making is": Stephen Nachmanovitch, *Free Play: Improvisation in Life and Art* (Los Angeles: Jeremy P. Tarcher, 1990), 99.

"I can tell you now": Kitty Grime, *Jazz Voices* (London: Quarter, 1983), 93.

"God has so arranged the body": 1 Corinthians 12:19–20, 24–26, NRSV.

"Beyond the aesthetic surprises": Nachmanovitch, *Free Play*, 96.

Pastor Gensel often went without: Edward Kennedy Ellington, *Music Is My Mistress* (New York: Da Capo, 1973), 282–285.

"His spectacular playing made me": From Wynton Marsalis's account of the event, online at https://wyntonmarsalis.org/blog/entry /visiting-the-great-clark-terry-in-the-hospital.

Clark blew out the candles: The moment has been captured online at https:// wyntonmarsalis.org/videos/view/happy-94th-birthday-clark-terry.

Noting how Clark's positive spirit: Marsalis, https://wyntonmarsalis.org /blog/entry/visiting-the-great-clark-terry-in-the-hospital.

CHAPTER TWELVE

I'll always be dedicating: Charlie Haden, quoted in *Rambling Boy*, a documentary directed by Reto Caduff. Timing: 1:23.

Don't ask what the world needs: Quoted by Gil Bailie, "In Gratitude," in *Violence Unveiled: Humanity at the Crossroads* (New York: Crossroad Publishing, 1995), xv.

All she knew was that: Personal conversation, July 19, 2021.

"A burning bush moment": Personal conversation, Rhinebeck, NY, August 25, 2013.

When his own moment of clarity came: McFerrin, personal conversation, Rhinebeck, NY, August 25, 2013.

"The two most important days": Matt Seybold, "The Apocryphal Twain: The Two Most Important Days of Your Life," blogpost on December 6, 2016, https://marktwainstudies.com.

"The first step of artistic growth": David Liebman, *Self-Portrait of a Jazz Artist: Musical Thoughts and Realities,* 2nd ed. (Rottenburg: Advance Press, 1996), 17–19.

Long before I met David: David Liebman, *Lookout Farm: A Case Study of Improvisation for Small Jazz Group* (Hollywood, CA: Alamo Publications, 1977).

"Working with Thelonious Monk": John Coltrane and Don DeMichael, "Coltrane on Coltrane," *Downbeat Magazine,* September 29, 1960, 26–27.

"He emptied himself": Philippians 2:7, NRSV.

"The Christ-life is the pattern": Kent Ira Groff, *Active Spirituality: A Guide for Seekers and Ministers* (Washington, DC: Alban Institute, 1993), 117.

The question is, How much: Giovanni Russonello, "Gary Peacock, Master Jazz Bassist, Is Dead at 85," *New York Times,* September 9, 2020, https://www.nytimes.com/2020/09/09/arts/music/gary-peacock-dead-at-85.html.

CHAPTER THIRTEEN

There is nothing irreligious in rhythm: Quoted by Helen Dance, "Has Jazz a Place in the Church," *Saturday Review,* July 15, 1967.

During his last semester of college: David Johnson, "Sacred Blue: Jazz Goes to Church in the 1960s," Indiana Public Media, December 23, 2019, https://indianapublicmedia.org/nightlights/sacred-blue-jazz-church-1960s.php.

His music received great reviews: Derick Cordoba, "Liturgical Jazz: The Lineage of the Subgenre in the Music of Edgar E. Summerlin" (PhD diss., Musical Arts in Music, University of Illinois at Urbana-Champaign, 2017).

He would later serve as the musical director: "The Upbeat Downbeat," episode on January 28, 1962, https://www.imdb.com/.

Williams's first religious composition: Jenny Gathright, "Shocking Omissions: Mary Lou Williams' Choral Masterpiece," August 7, 2017, https://www.npr.org/2017/08/07/541822331/shocking-omissions-mary-lou-williams-choral-masterpiece-black-christ-of-the-ande.

"Let not your heart be troubled": John 14:1, KJV.

"These concerts are not the traditional": Ellington, *Music Is My Mistress,* 267–268.

"We think the man himself": Vaughn A. Booker, *Lift Every Voice and Swing: Black Musicians and Religious Culture in the Jazz Century* (New York: New York University Press, 2020), 148.

"We don't like what you're doing": Derrick Bang, *Vince Guaraldi at the Piano* (Jefferson, NC: McFarland, 2012), 155.

"they were petty and difficult": Bang, *Vince Guaraldi at the Piano*, 156.

I preached the sermon: This is the improvisation that follows this chapter. It was composed on the plane to San Francisco.

Jim's trio and choir: Derrick Bang offers a full report of the event in his blog, at http://impressionsofvince.blogspot.com/2015/08/an-afternoon-of -grace.html, along with a later report of the September 2015 presentation of the full mass in Clarks Summit, PA. Derrick also requested that I provide regular reports of the transcription process, which appear in postings in June, July, and August 2015 on his blog.

What I have learned about jazz: A report of the Pennsylvania event appears on the website of the Presbyterian Church (USA) news, https://www.pcusa .org/news/2015/9/9/all-jazz-celebrating-50th-anniversary-first-us-jaz/.

CHAPTER FOURTEEN

I believe in the ultimate victory: Dave Brubeck, "The Ultimate Victory of Faith, Hope, and Love," for the "This I Believe" series on National Public Radio, June 13, 2005. Text online at https://www.npr.org/templates/story /story.php?storyId=4698339.

My life flows on in endless song: Robert Lowry, "How Can I Keep from Singing," public domain, 1868.

"Listen to that": *The Genius of Bud Powell*, liner notes, Gary Giddins, Verve Records, 1976.

"The thing that attracted me": Maurice Hines, *Erroll Garner: No One Can Hear You Read*, directed by Atticus Brady. First Run Features, 2012, www .firstrunfeatures.com.

"I noticed that one word—joy": "Family and Friends Celebrate Dave Brubeck's Life," Associated Press, May 12, 2013.

"The Lord is the Spirit": 2 Corinthians 3:17, NRSV.

its most distinctive character: Lesslie Newbigin, *The Gospel in a Pluralistic Society* (Grand Rapids, MI: Eerdmans, 1989), 227–228.

"All people that on earth": William Kethe, "Old Hundredth," 1560, public domain.